Beyond These Walls

Beyond These Walls

Matilde Hernandez

Copyright © 2025 Matilde Hernandez. All rights reserved.

No part of this publication may be reproduced, stored in a retrieval system or transmitted in any form or by any means, electronic, mechanical, photocopying, recording or otherwise, without prior permission of Halo Publishing International.

The views and opinions expressed in this book are those of the author and do not necessarily reflect the official policy or position of Halo Publishing International. Any content provided by our authors are of their opinion and are not intended to malign any religion, ethnic group, club, organization, company, individual or anyone or anything.

No generative artificial intelligence (AI) was used in the writing of this work. The author expressly prohibits any entity from using this publication to train AI technologies to generate text, including, without limitation, technologies capable of generating works in the same style or genre as this publication.

For permission requests, write to the publisher, addressed "Attention: Permissions Coordinator," at the address below.

Halo Publishing International
7550 W IH-10 #800, PMB 2069,
San Antonio, TX 78229

First Edition, January 2025
ISBN: 978-1-63765-592-4

The information contained within this book is strictly for informational purposes. Unless otherwise indicated, all the names, characters, businesses, places, events and incidents in this book are either the product of the author's imagination or used in a fictitious manner. Any resemblance to actual persons, living or dead, or actual events is purely coincidental.

Halo Publishing International is a self-publishing company that publishes adult fiction and non-fiction, children's literature, self-help, spiritual, and faith-based books. We continually strive to help authors reach their publishing goals and provide many different services that help them do so. We do not publish books that are deemed to be politically, religiously, or socially disrespectful, or books that are sexually provocative, including erotica. Halo reserves the right to refuse publication of any manuscript if it is deemed not to be in line with our principles. Do you have a book idea you would like us to consider publishing? Please visit www.halopublishing.com for more information.

I am deeply grateful for all the experiences, the ups and downs, and the twists and turns that have been part of my journey so far. My gratitude extends first and foremost to God, whose strength and light guided me through my darkest moments.

To my Madre—your unwavering support was my anchor, guiding me through the toughest moments and showing me how to keep moving forward with strength and grace. I could not have raised my children without you by my side.

This book is dedicated to my children. I am overjoyed and honored that God chose me to be your mother. Thank you for inspiring me to grow and evolve, for your unwavering love and support. As parents, we don't have a blueprint for raising or caring for our children. Still, God allows us to improve continually, cultivate a greater sense of self-compassion and forgiveness, and the opportunity to rewrite our stories! I love you dearly.

Understanding ourselves is a gradual process—one that requires introspection, unpacking past traumas, and releasing judgments and noise that may have clouded our path. Forgiveness for ourselves and others liberates us from our past and opens the door to a life filled with joy and possibility. Do not be afraid to start over; it's an opportunity to build something even better.

Remember that people are not interested in sitting with the great; they are interested in sitting with the broken and giving them a word of encouragement or helping them up. You wield the power to choose what you react to; let go of anything that impedes your happiness.

You deserve a happy, healthy, and whole life. Be kind to yourself, always forgive yourself, and learn from everything life throws at you – for nothing in this world is without purpose.

Love Mom.

I also want to express my gratitude to the angels God placed in my life—those who walked beside me as I healed. I am so thankful for your unwavering support, prayers, and belief in me, even when I couldn't see my worth. To my friends, I could not have made it this far without your support. I love you dearly, and not one day goes by without me praying for you and thanking God for our encounters.

CONTENTS

INTRODUCTION   11

CHAPTER 1

Understanding the Power of Personal Narrative in Shaping Identity   15

CHAPTER 2

Acknowledging Your Past: It's the place where we should forgive ourselves!   23

   The Art of fostering self-compassion and forgiveness   29

   The journey towards healing   34

CHAPTER 3

Beyond These Walls   37
   A guiding light   39

CHAPTER 4

Okay, it happened. Now what?   45
   Separation brings appreciation   50
   Live again and learn from the lessons   54
   Grow Through What You Go Through....   59

CHAPTER 5

The Challenges of Re-entry   61

CHAPTER 6

Embracing Inner Healing and Renewal   69
What do you have to let go of?
Embracing Freedom and Resilience Beyond the Walls   73

Life is a unique journey for each of us.
Let's make the most of it — 77

TIME TO REFLECT AND JOURNAL... — 81

CHAPTER 7
Despite the detours, I am ready to take on another live event with renewed determination — 95

> Doubt is the enemy of hope — 102

CHAPTER 8
The Invisible Bars — 107

> Finding Freedom: Navigating the Mental Landscape of Incarceration — 111

CHAPTER 9
Dare 2 Lift It: Finding Freedom Within — 115

> Resources for Healing and Rebuilding — 118

CHAPTER 10
"Are You Ready for a Fresh Start?" — 125

> Let It Go — 133

> Exercises — 139

> Here are some tips for living a fulfilling and balanced life — 141

MINDFULNESS MOMENTS
Closing the Chapter: Beyond the Walls — 145

MEET THE AUTHOR — 155
LET'S CONNECT — 157

INTRODUCTION

You owe it to yourself to break free from the past and live a happy, healthy, successful life. Let us shift from merely existing to actively thriving in life's abundance. You deserve to liberate yourself from the past and welcome a life filled with happiness, health, and success. Let's begin to flourish in the richness of life.

Life is indeed a journey and as you navigate it, be sure to live authentically, saying farewell to shame and breaking through any barriers by living it fully. Every obstacle encountered along the way is only a detour designed to transform you into the best version of yourself. You were born to make an impact, to transform lives, and to add value to this world.

Some adversities make us hide and feel shame and self-doubt. As a high school dropout and young mother, I felt lost. But we all hold immense potential. I had just earned my GED and started college when I moved to Georgia. I wanted to show my kids and myself that getting knocked down doesn't mean you have to stay there. Keep going, and rise stronger.

At the end of 2007, I found myself in a difficult situation, and that is when my journey truly started: a period of isolation, growth, healing, and lots of questions. I asked myself how I had reached this point, leaving everything behind and separating from my kids and those I was so connected to. So, there I was, forced to sit by myself, and that is when my journey beyond those figurative walls began.

In this new place, there was so much revelation about what I felt was holding me back. I began dismantling the trauma of life, my decision-making, and family dynamics. I never thought I'd make a decision that would result in confinement, but I did make the best out of it—seeing how so many people are able to enter a facility and make it their home opened my eyes. Not only are these places home to some who don't have the support they need to deal with their addiction and pain, but they are also a temporary home for those who make decisions that could land them in prison.

Welcome to "Beyond These Walls: Breakthroughs for Hope, Joy, and Growth," a guide for those reentering society after incarceration. This book emphasizes setting boundaries, living authentically, and cultivating a growth mindset. I'm Matilde Hernandez, a Personal Growth and Wellness coach committed to helping individuals reach their maximum potential and enhance their well-being, regardless of background.

This book offers hope, direction, and practical strategies for overcoming obstacles and achieving a fulfilling life during the challenging reintegration process, whether you're newly released, a young parent, or dealing with divorce or poor decisions.

This often comes with its own set of internal struggles, including mental health issues stemming from trauma, anxiety, and sadness. These obstacles may create additional challenges that impede an individual's capacity to reintegrate into society properly. Through the insights shared, we seek to inspire those on the journey to reentry to overcome challenges and build a better future.

While the reintegration process might be complex, it is essential to realize that there is hope for a brighter future outside of these walls. I want to extend my utmost gratitude in this book to the people who have served as my support pillars—friends I don't have to name, whose unwavering presence has accompanied me through ups and downs over the past eight years. They have been there during my struggles, helping me find meaning in the chaos I will now share with the world.

To my Children, as we continue to journey together in this life, I acknowledge that sometimes we will be challenged, shifted, and internally frustrated with ourselves. Understanding ourselves takes time, unpacking the trauma, silencing the noise of judgment, and forgiving ourselves to release it all and embrace the promise of a life filled with joy, freedom, and inner peace.

Despite the challenges and the moments when we've kept ourselves hidden, we deserve to reclaim our lives and live authentically. I want this book to serve as a beacon of light to guide you when the days become dark, to remind you that it is not how you start but how you finish—fulfilling all that God has bestowed upon you. Live your life freely, and help others by sharing your story.

Remember, your environment does not determine your worth or limit your potential. By cultivating a positive mindset, setting goals, seeking positive influences, and taking the initiative in creating opportunities, you can maximize your full potential despite any external constraints. Beyond These Walls offers further guidance, strategies, and inspiring quotes to help you navigate these challenges and unleash your true potential.

CHAPTER 1

Understanding the Power of Personal Narrative in Shaping Identity

---

Within the chapters of our lives, the significance of one's story is not just a narrative; it's a transformative force shaping the essence of our identity. Embrace the power of your story, for it holds the key to unlocking your true potential and illuminating the path beyond these walls. Our good and bad experiences impact how we perceive ourselves and the world. Our self-image, values, beliefs, and attitudes are influenced by how we perceive and comprehend our experiences. For instance, individuals who have been through profound hardships, such as incarceration, may experience emotions such as shame, remorse, and diminished self-worth. These encounters have the potential to mold their identity and impact how they interact with others and approach life. On the other hand, positive experiences, such as professional or personal successes, can also help form one's identity, fostering self-confidence and a favorable self-image.

Furthermore, the way we express our story has a significant impact on our identity. Our choice of language and how we present our experiences can influence self-perception and others' perceptions of us. For example, someone who frames their jail experience as a learning opportunity and a chance for personal improvement may have a more positive self-image and view on life. Taking ownership of one's narrative and actively reinventing it may be a potent tool for creating one's identity. We may alter how we view ourselves and our role in the world by recognizing the past and finding meaning in our experiences. We can concentrate on our strengths and tell ourselves a more optimistic story. Our story has a massive impact on our identity. I remember when I felt that all the walls were closing in, I was grappling with feeling disappointed and losing hope. During this period, I realized the importance of how we talk to ourselves, realizing that our thoughts can determine our bounce back from life's challenges.

Our good and bad experiences impact how we perceive ourselves and the world around us. Taking ownership of our stories and actively reframing them may be an excellent tool for changing our identities and building a more positive narrative for ourselves. Our narrative is more than simply the recounting of events that happened to us; it is a lens through which we make sense of our experiences and comprehend our place in the world. It reflects our perspective on ourselves, our relationships, and our future. Our narrative is not set in stone but instead evolves as we learn new things and mature as people. The way we tell our stories may have a significant influence on our mental and emotional health. We may create a poor self-image and battle with emotions of low self-worth and pessimism if we choose to concentrate on the negative parts of our experiences. However, by focusing on the positive elements of our experiences and seeing challenges as chances for development and learning, we may build a more positive self-image and optimism for the future.

> *"How we tell our stories influences how others perceive us. We may seem pessimistic and gloomy if we consistently focus on the negative aspects of our experiences. Conversely, if we choose to concentrate on the positive parts and present them in a way that encourages growth and learning, we may come across as resilient and optimistic. Taking control of our stories and actively reshaping them can be a powerful tool for changing our identities and creating a more positive narrative for ourselves. By acknowledging the past and emphasizing our strengths, we can change the way we see ourselves and our role in the world and tell ourselves a more optimistic story."*

There is a need to redefine one's story after life's challenges. It might be difficult to move forward after facing incarceration or other severe life obstacles.

Without addressing the impact these events have had on our sense of self and outlook on life, we risk being left with powerlessness, despair, and uncertainty about our next steps. However, we can change our story and write a new narrative that stresses development, resilience, and optimism. This process may include reevaluating our views and values, acknowledging our strengths and flaws, and attempting to make sense of our experiences. For example, if someone has been incarcerated, they may feel shame or remorse, which may have a severe effect on their self-worth and confidence. To rewrite their new narrative, they must recognize these emotions and reframe their experiences as opportunities for personal development and change. By focusing on their progress since their imprisonment, they may develop a more positive narrative for themselves and shape their identity accordingly.

Similarly, those who have faced significant hardships, such as a major illness or the death of a loved one, can benefit from reframing their narrative to find meaning in their experience and articulate how they have evolved. This process may include investigating their ideas and values, evaluating their talents and shortcomings, and determining how they may utilize their expertise to serve others. The desire to rewrite one's narrative after any shift to other major life problems is critical for moving forward and constructing a brighter future. By understanding the impact of our experiences and actively striving to build a new narrative for ourselves, we may mold our identity in a positive light and find hope for the future.

After imprisonment or severe other life obstacles, the urge to rewrite our narrative is often essential for personal development and healing. These encounters may profoundly influence our sense of self, relationships, and attitude toward life, which, left unaddressed, may lead to feelings of hopelessness, loneliness, and despair. We must first recognize and embrace the event's significance to rewrite our narrative. This may include dealing with harsh feelings, such as shame, guilt, or trauma. It is essential to understand that these feelings are normal and that seeking help from others, such as friends, family, or a therapist, is OK.

Following that, we must recognize and challenge any negative attitudes or thoughts holding us back. For example, individuals who have been incarcerated may think that they are unworthy of love or success because of their past mistakes. It is crucial to question these ideas by uncovering evidence to the contrary to reframe the narrative in a more positive perspective. This might include focusing on their personal growth since their sentence or acknowledging the lessons they have learned.

Moreover, reimagining one's story often requires acknowledging both strengths and flaws. This process can be empowering and contribute to developing confidence and resilience. It may involve focusing on personal growth, such as acquiring new skills or establishing meaningful connections, and then taking tangible steps to achieve these aspirations. Ultimately, uncovering the significance of one's experiences is essential for reframing one's narrative. This may involve recognizing how adversity has positively shaped them, fostering empathy, and utilizing their expertise to support others through volunteering or advocacy.

Restructuring one's life story after incarceration or other major life challenges can be an incredibly transformative and healing experience. It demands great courage, deep self-reflection, and a genuine willingness to confront damaging beliefs and embrace personal growth and change. By acknowledging our past mistakes and actively working to construct a more positive narrative for ourselves, we can profoundly reshape our identity in a compassionate and meaningful way.

Embracing the Significance of Your Story:

To embark on the transformative journey of rewriting your narrative, it is crucial to deeply acknowledge and embrace the profound significance of the events that have unfolded in your life. This profound recognition is not a surrender to adversity but an empowering declaration of authorship over your own story. It requires facing and addressing challenging emotions directly—such as feelings of shame, guilt, and trauma. While these emotions may seem formidable, they are intrinsic and valuable components woven into the fabric of your personal experience.

Seeking Help and Embracing Support:

Understanding that it's alright to seek help is not just a sign of strength but a testament to your resilience. Reach out to the pillars of your support system—be it friends, family, or a therapist. Their understanding and empathy can serve as a soothing balm, helping you navigate the labyrinth of emotions. It takes immense courage to share your vulnerability, but in doing so, you allow others to walk this transformative journey alongside you.

Moving Forward Together:

This chapter serves as a guiding light, illuminating the path toward embracing hope after life's trials. By acknowledging your story's significance, confronting difficult emotions, and seeking support, you pave the way for profound healing and transformation. Together, we will navigate the complexities of rewriting your narrative, uncovering the resilience that resides within you, and emerging not as a prisoner of the past but as a pioneer of your future. Beyond these walls, a new story awaits—one of strength, redemption, and boundless possibilities.

By acknowledging the profound significance of your story, facing difficult emotions head-on, and seeking the necessary support, you are laying the groundwork for profound healing and transformation. Together, we will adeptly navigate the complexities of rewriting your narrative, unveiling the resilience that lies within you. You will emerge not as a prisoner of the past but as a pioneer of your future. Beyond these walls lies a new story characterized by strength, redemption, and boundless possibilities.

CHAPTER 2

Acknowledging Your Past: It's the place where we should forgive ourselves!

---

*"Forgiveness is not an occasional act;
it is a constant attitude."*
- Martin Luther King Jr.

In rewriting your narrative, acknowledging your past is not merely a step; it's a profound pilgrimage—a journey back to the origins of your strength and the roots of your resilience. It's an odyssey that demands the most potent healing elixir: forgiveness, especially towards oneself. It is critical to recognize and embrace your history before moving forward and rewriting your narrative. This entails dealing with tough feelings and memories, such as shame, guilt, or trauma. While recognizing your history may be difficult, it is a necessary step toward healing and rehabilitation. By facing your past, you may better understand how your prior experiences have impacted your sense of self and attitude toward life. You may begin to take charge of your narrative and work toward a more positive future.

Here are some techniques for dealing with your past:

- **Practice self-compassion**: It is important to be kind and compassionate to yourself while you address tough feelings and memories. Practice self-compassion by admitting that your experiences were painful and that it is natural to have unpleasant sentiments

- **Seek assistance:** Don't hesitate to contact others while you come to terms with your history. Speaking with a therapist, joining a support group, or confiding in a trusted friend or family member can be incredibly beneficial.

- **Reflect on your prior experiences:** Take the time to consider your past experiences and how they have influenced your sense of self and view on life. Consider how your experiences have shaped your views and values and identify any opposing thoughts or beliefs preventing you from moving forward. Practice mindfulness: Mindfulness can help you remain present and focused when confronted with uncomfortable emotions or experiences. Focus on your breath or participate in other grounding activities to help you practice mindfulness.

- **Utilize writing:** Writing is a wonderful tool for addressing your history. Consider keeping a diary or expressing yourself creatively via writing to gain insight into your past and work toward a more positive future..

Understanding the role of past decisions and experiences

Understanding the impact of prior actions and experiences is crucial in rewriting your narrative and moving ahead after incarceration or other severe life problems. While our prior actions and experiences may have a big influence on our self-esteem, view of life, values, and actions, it is important to understand that our previous choices and experiences do not define us. By recognizing the impact of our prior actions and experiences, we may begin to take responsibility for our narrative and progress toward a more positive future.

Here are some techniques for comprehending the significance of previous choices and experiences:

Look for patterns in your previous choices and experiences. Consider if any repeating themes or habits have affected your present circumstance.

- **Recognize the influence of other factors**: Our previous decisions and experiences are not always the consequence of our choices. Recognize the impact of external elements on your prior experiences, such as systemic difficulties or environmental concerns.
- **Identify development opportunities**: Examine your prior experiences for potential personal growth and development areas. Consider how you have grown and learned from

previous errors and any qualities or abilities you have gained.

- **It is essential to question negative beliefs:** Identify contradicting evidence and reframe your experiences in a more positive perspective to effectively challenge any negative assumptions and cognitive patterns that past experiences may have created.

- **Use your prior experiences to motivate yourself**: Utilize the power of your past experiences to ignite your motivation. Allow the lessons learned, obstacles overcome, and accomplishments achieved to propel you toward your current goals. Remember, your past triumphs are a testament to your strength, which you can use to overcome any challenges that come your way.

Overcoming denial and shame

Overcoming denial and guilt is an essential step in redefining your narrative and moving ahead after incarceration or other major life setbacks. Denial and shame may impede healing and progress, but there are techniques for overcoming them. In the tapestry of healing, acknowledging and overcoming denial and guilt are pivotal threads. These emotions can act as heavy anchors, weighing down the spirit and hindering the process of reshaping narratives. Denial, with its deceptive allure of protection, shields us from the harsh truths of our past.

It whispers in our ears, urging us to minimize the impact of prior events. Yet, within denial's grasp, the potential for growth remains stifled, hidden beneath layers of avoidance.

Denial is a protective mechanism that often leads us to deny or minimize the influence of prior events. It may be easy to avoid addressing tough feelings and experiences, but doing so will impede our progress and prevent us from making meaningful life changes.

Facing denial is akin to stepping into the light after a long, shadowy journey. It requires courage, an unwavering commitment to truth, and an acceptance of the past, no matter how painful. Addressing the tough feelings and experiences that denial seeks to conceal is not a sign of weakness but a testament to your strength. It's important to acknowledge that real progress starts when you face the truth about your past. Denial might feel like protection, but it hinders the transformative healing you deserve.

Shame is another complex emotion characterized by feelings of inadequacy, unworthiness, or guilt, which may lead to feelings of isolation and despair and can also be a substantial impediment to healing and progress.

However, within the depths of shame lies an opportunity for profound liberation. Acknowledging shame and understanding its roots are the first steps toward breaking the chains that have bound your spirit for too long. It's about more than just recognizing the pain—it's about refusing to be defined by it. Confronting shame is a courageous act of rebellion against the self-condemnation that has held you captive. By doing so, you make a powerful declaration: Your worth is inherent, unshakable, and beyond the reach of any past mistakes or judgments.

Here are some techniques for dealing with denial and shame:

- **Practice self-compassion:** It is essential to be kind and compassionate to yourself while addressing tough feelings and memories. Practice self-compassion by acknowledging that your experiences were painful and having unpleasant feelings is natural.

- **Seek assistance:** Seek the guidance of a therapist or counselor. Professional support provides a safe space to navigate the complexities of denial and shame, offering insights and techniques for healing.

- **Identify and address negative ideas:** Negative beliefs and thought patterns can promote denial and shame. Identify and confront these ideas by gathering alternative information and reframing your experience more positively. Exercise using positive affirmations to help fight negative ideas and cognitive patterns. Practice telling yourself affirmations such as "I am worthy of love and respect" or "I am capable of creating a positive future for myself."

- **Engage in self-care activities:** Engage in regular self-care activities such as exercise, meditation, or spending time in nature can help to lessen feelings of shame and denial and encourage Healing.
- **Healthy eating:** Nourishing your body with nutritious foods can positively impact your mental health.
- **Connecting with loved ones:** Spending time with supportive friends and family members.
- **Setting boundaries:** Learning to say no and prioritizing your needs.
- **Embracing vulnerability:** Embrace vulnerability as a strength, not a weakness. By sharing your struggles, you invite others to share theirs, fostering connection and understanding. This mutual openness creates a space where healing and growth flourish.

The Art of fostering self-compassion and forgiveness

As you step into this new chapter of life, it is vital to equip yourself with the tools that will help you heal, grow, and thrive. Self-compassion and forgiveness stand out as powerful allies in rewriting your narrative and finding hope after incarceration or any significant life struggle. These practices aren't just concepts—they are lifelines that will guide you toward a future filled with possibility.

Self-Compassion: The Gateway to Healing

Being self-compassionate means treating yourself with the same kindness and understanding that you would offer to a dear friend. It's about embracing your humanity, acknowledging that everyone makes mistakes, and offering yourself grace instead of harsh judgment.

When I began to practice self-compassion, it transformed the way I viewed my past decisions. Instead of seeing them as permanent failures, I started to understand them as choices made in a specific season of my life, influenced by circumstances and emotions that were beyond my control. This shift in perspective is essential—it helps to quiet the inner critic and opens the door to healing.

For those who have experienced the pain of incarceration or other traumatic life events, self-compassion can be the antidote to guilt and self-blame. These emotions often linger long after the event has passed, chaining you to a past that no longer serves you. But, through self-compassion, you can begin to dismantle those chains, allowing yourself the freedom to move forward without the weight of regret.

Forgiveness: Releasing the Past to Embrace the Future

Equally important on your journey is the practice of forgiveness. Forgiveness is not about condoning the wrongs that have been done—whether by others or by yourself—but about choosing to release the bitterness and resentment that keep you trapped in a cycle of pain. It's about reclaiming your power and saying, "I will not let the past define me or dictate my future."

Forgiving others can be challenging, especially if their actions have left deep scars. Yet, holding onto anger only prolongs your suffering. When you choose to forgive, you free yourself from the toxic grip of resentment, allowing space for peace and growth to take root.

Forgiving yourself is perhaps even more critical. We all have moments we wish we could erase, decisions we regret, and words we wish we could take back. But it's important to remember that your worth is not diminished by your mistakes. By forgiving yourself, you acknowledge that you are more than the sum of your past actions—you are a person deserving of love, redemption, and a bright future.

Moving Forward: Embracing Your New Narrative

As you integrate self-compassion and forgiveness into your daily life, you begin to rewrite your story. You are no longer defined by the chapters that came before. Instead, you become the author of a new narrative—one in which you are resilient, empowered, and filled with hope.

This journey will not be without its challenges, but every step you take towards self-compassion and forgiveness is a step towards freedom. It's a journey worth taking, and it's yours to embrace fully. Your past is part of your story, but it does not have to be your future. As you move forward, carry these tools with you, and allow them to guide you to the life you truly deserve.

Techniques for Cultivating Self-Compassion and Forgiveness

As you continue your journey of healing and personal growth, it's important to develop habits that nurture your inner strength and resilience. Self-compassion and forgiveness are foundational practices that can help you break free from the past and embrace a future filled with hope and possibility. Here are some empowering techniques to help you cultivate these life-changing habits:

1. **Practice Self-Acceptance:** Begin by accepting yourself exactly as you are—flaws, strengths, and all. Understand that you are a work in progress, and that's perfectly okay. Embrace your imperfections as part of your unique journey and recognize that you are doing your best given your circumstances. When you accept yourself fully, you create a safe space in which growth and transformation can flourish.

2. **Reframe Negative Self-Talk:** Your inner dialogue has a profound impact on how you perceive yourself and the world around you. Instead of indulging in self-criticism, consciously choose to reframe your thoughts to be more compassionate and forgiving. Focus on your strengths, achievements, and the lessons you've learned along the way. Treat

yourself with the same kindness and empathy that you would offer to a close friend. Remember, mistakes are simply stepping stones on the path to growth—they don't define your worth.

3. **Accept Responsibility, but Don't Dwell on It:** Taking responsibility for your past actions is a crucial step in your healing process, but it's equally important to understand that those actions do not define who you are today. Acknowledge any past mistakes, learn from them, and then release the burden of guilt and shame. Forgiveness, both for yourself and others, is key to letting go of anger and resentment. By doing so, you free yourself from the chains of the past and open up to a more positive and empowered future.

4. **Forgive to Free Yourself:** Forgiveness is not about excusing what has happened; it's about freeing yourself from the emotional weight of those experiences. Holding onto anger, bitterness, or regret only keeps you tethered to a past you cannot change. By practicing forgiveness, you reclaim your peace and create space for new beginnings. Forgive yourself for past regrets and understand that you are worthy of moving forward with a renewed sense of purpose and optimism.

5. **Be Patient and Gentle with Yourself:** Cultivating self-compassion and forgiveness is

a journey, not a destination. It's important to remember that these practices take time and persistence. There will be days when it feels easier, and days when it feels impossible—and that is okay. Be patient and gentle with yourself throughout the process. Growth takes time, and every small step forward is progress. Trust in your ability to shape your own destiny and know that you have the strength within to overcome any obstacle.

Encouraging Quote:

"Your journey is not about perfection, but about progress. Every time you choose compassion over criticism, forgiveness over resentment, you evolve into a stronger, more resilient version of yourself."
– Unknown

The journey towards healing

In the chapters, we will explore these techniques in depth, guiding you on the transformative journey of overcoming denial and shame. Remember, the process may be arduous, but with each step, you shatter the barriers that have held you captive. Embrace your vulnerability, for it holds the seeds of immense strength. Together, we will illuminate the path to healing, nurturing the roots of resilience and self-acceptance and paving the way for a future unburdened by the weight of denial and shame.

The powerful quote by Martin Luther King Jr. that I shared at the beginning of this chapter encapsulates the essence of forgiveness as a continuous, transformative process rather than a one-time event. It speaks to the enduring strength and openness of heart required to embrace forgiveness as a way of life, highlighting its profound impact on both the forgiver and the forgiven.

CHAPTER 3

Beyond These Walls

"Every adversity, every failure, every heartache carries with it the seed of an equal or greater benefit."
- **Napoleon Hill**

In the intricate web of life's unforeseen twists and turns, it's common to experience a sense of entrapment within our own minds, constructing barriers that echo our feelings of isolation and despair. Reflecting on the year 2007, I found myself grappling with this suffocating reality. My life underwent a sudden and unexpected shift, resembling a detour that I feared would lead to a point of no return. This dramatic change was propelled by a series of decisions, some wise and some not, ultimately shaping my world into an uncertain and claustrophobic existence.

We often find ourselves erecting emotional fortresses brick by brick, with each misstep in life serving as mortar, effectively sealing us off from hope and light. Despite being immersed in this disheartening state, I've come to recognize that even during our darkest moments, there lies a profound significance. Understanding that everything ultimately serves a higher purpose, guided by faith and perseverance, offers a source of comfort. Embracing this perspective, we can break down these self-imposed barriers and emerge into the light once more.

It was a brief misstep, a fleeting moment of poor judgment in what had otherwise been a journey of growth and self-improvement. I was so close to completing my bachelor's degree—a milestone that stood as a testament to my resilience and unyielding determination. Yet, while I was achieving this academic success, I was also fighting an internal battle, wrestling with the shadows of mental health challenges that threatened to dim my light. Despite these struggles, I held fast to a vision of a brighter future for my family. My decision to leave Florida wasn't just about changing our location; it was about carving out a new path, one where education would be the foundation for a better life for my children. It was a choice made with hope in my heart, a belief that no matter how hard the journey became, we were moving toward something greater.

But life's journey is unpredictable. It reshapes our plans and challenges our very essence. What I didn't realize then was that within the confines of my circumstances, I would discover a strength I never knew I had. What began as a painful experience became the catalyst for my transformation. Behind closed doors and within the shadows of regret, I found an unwavering resolve—a glimmer of light that illuminated even the darkest corners of my existence.

I realized that the walls surrounding me, whether tangible or of the mind, could be dismantled.

This chapter is both my story and a testament to the human spirit's capacity to endure, adapt, and overcome. Even in the depths of confinement, whether literal or figurative, there lies a latent strength waiting to be uncovered. By sharing my journey, I want to impart the truth that these walls are not insurmountable.

Together, we'll uncover the path to rebuilding lives, reclaiming identities, and basking in the light beyond these seemingly impenetrable walls. In the labyrinth of darkness, where every corner seems to echo with the ghosts of our past mistakes, it's essential to recognize that the walls we build are not impenetrable fortresses. They are constructions of our own making, shaped by experiences, regret, and fear. As I navigated my labyrinth, I discovered that within these walls resides a potential for transformation as vast as the universe itself.

A guiding light

In the words of Maya Angelou, "You may encounter many defeats, but you must not be defeated."

Your past, no matter how challenging, does not dictate your future. Each step you take towards rewriting your narrative is a victory—a testament to your strength and determination. The process may be arduous, but the promise of renewal and rediscovery lies within it.

Finding hope as you persevere:

Life cannot be measured by the number of breaths we take, the pain we experience, or even the goodness we accumulate. It's about learning to appreciate every day, seeing ourselves as valuable individuals, regardless of any changes in our lives. We must learn to break free from self-judgment and embrace growth, even in the most challenging circumstances. Anxiety may arise when facing life's obstacles, and the opinions of others can make us doubt ourselves and our ability to start anew. But we must not lose hope or give up, for in every setback lies an opportunity to gain experience, share, and inspire others. We must keep moving forward, remembering that everything has a purpose and trusting that a higher power guides our journey. So, let's live for today, keep our heads up, and embrace the twists and turns of life with faith and perseverance.

Embracing Self-Value:

Amidst the clamor of self-doubt, it is crucial to recognize our intrinsic value. Each of us is a unique thread in the grand tapestry of existence, contributing a hue and pattern only we can offer. Our journey, with all its twists and turns, does not diminish our worth; it enriches the tapestry, making it a vivid and extraordinary masterpiece. In the dance of life, perseverance is the rhythm that keeps us moving forward. Despite adversity, we must not lose hope or surrender to the weight of challenges. Each step, no matter how small, is a testament to our courage and determination. The setbacks, the challenges, the moments of despair—all contribute to shaping our resilience and wisdom. These trials refine us, not define us, revealing our inherent strength and worth. Embrace the uncertainties with faith, knowing the power to navigate life's storms lies within you. We recognize that we deserve hope, joy, and success by valuing ourselves. In each moment, let's hold our heads high, share our light, and become a beacon of hope for others. In the warm embrace of self-value, we find the strength to persevere and the courage to face our journey with gratitude and optimism.

Breaking free into a better you:

Reset your mindset, embrace confidence, and lighten up - these are the words we hear, but do we say those things to ourselves? Our inner dialogue can keep us captives, preventing us from forgiving ourselves, showing up for ourselves, or even being kind to ourselves. However, detours in life are not meant to punish or trap us in a place where there's no way out. They are opportunities for development, places where you can learn to change your mindset, to outgrow the old patterns, to outgrow the old pain.

In this chapter, I want to guide you to a place where you will break free and live the life you were destined to live, forgiving yourself and others who judged you without understanding. The secret sauce for transformation is in you, a gift waiting to be cultivated. Forgiving ourselves is essential to reconnecting with our true essence.

Take a moment to reflect on your life. Many drift through life, hoping things will magically improve – more time, money, friends, a better lifestyle, family, spouse, career, or job. However, the first step is to assess what no longer serves us, what relationships need to be released, and who we need to become to reach our full potential. It will not be easy, but it will be worth it. Remember that the journey is not about dragging everybody along; it's about embracing, learning, living, and sharing your unique path with others.

A journey of self-liberation and transformation:

In the gentle cadence of life, the phrases "reset your mindset, embrace confidence, and lighten up" often grace our ears, yet we seldom extend these affirmations to the most crucial audience: ourselves. Within the symphony of our thoughts, our inner noise can become a captive force, preventing us from powerful acts of self-forgiveness, self-acknowledgment, and self-kindness. This chapter invites us to explore the profound journey of breaking free from the walls that limit us from living the life destined for us.

Nurturing inner harmony:

Imagine a space where every thought is a note in a melody of self-compassion. In this warm embrace, the words we often hear become affirmations we speak to ourselves daily. It's a sanctuary where our inner noise transforms into a harmonious rhythm, allowing forgiveness and kindness to flourish.

Detours: the landscape of personal growth:

Detours in life are not punitive measures; they are landscapes of development. Rather than seeing them as obstacles, view them as opportunities to gain experience, grow, and anchor yourself in the knowledge that development is an integral part of the human journey. In these detours, the seeds of transformation are planted, enabling us to outgrow old patterns and pains, steering our walk toward the authentic direction of our soul. I encourage you to continue to be your true self, spread light in every room you enter, and keep your head up, knowing that you are destined for more.

Cultivating the gift within:

Within each of us resides a unique gift — a set of seeds waiting to be cultivated. It's a precious endowment bestowed upon us. Cultivation takes time, and forgiveness is the nourishment that allows our true essence to flourish. Take stock of your life, not as a critical assessment but as a loving journey into self-discovery, identifying elements that no longer serve your evolution. God created one of you. The world is waiting for you. Break free and be the best you.

CHAPTER 4

Okay, it happened. Now what?

"Until you make peace with who you are, you'll never be content with what you have."
- Doris Mortma"

Many find themselves at a juncture where introspection prompts questions such as, "How did I get here? What happened?" These queries reverberate with the echoes of untold stories and unexplored depths. Yet, in the tapestry of human experience, the real challenge is not deciphering the past but responding to the present with a resounding "Now what? Where do we go from here?" Life, an ever-unfolding narrative, doesn't pause for our contemplation. It propels forward, unyielding and relentless. The direction it takes is intricately woven into our interactions — with ourselves, others, and the circumstances we navigate. It beckons us to decode the factors that anchor us and those that hold us back. Acknowledging the reality that we can't erase the footprints of our past is the first step. However, more crucial is the recognition of our inherent strengths. Often overlooked in the shadow of setbacks, these strengths become the building blocks for a resilient foundation. This foundation is not a fortress to hide within but a stage to stand tall, unburdened, and unafraid.

Embracing life after the unforeseen: What's next?

"You may not be able to rewrite the chapters that have already been penned, but remember, you can shape the narrative moving forward. This crucial stage demands a profound exploration of the self - uncovering your strengths, identifying the obstacles, and building an unwavering foundation. This foundation is not rooted in regrets but in recognizing the inner resilience that has weathered the storms of life.

No longer hiding:

The foundation you create should be a sanctuary where you no longer need to hide. It's a space of self-acceptance where the scars of the past are embraced as badges of resilience. Now that it has happened, the journey is not about concealing but about revealing—exposing the authentic self to possibilities.

Openness to a new future:

This newly laid foundation serves as a launching pad for the future. It's a place where you become open to life's infinite possibilities. The "Now what?" becomes an exciting exploration, an invitation to co-author a new chapter filled with resilience, self-love, and intentional living.

Healing and intentional living:

It becomes our responsibility to embark on a journey of healing. Healing is not about erasing the past but about understanding it, learning from it, and allowing it to shape a more resilient version of ourselves. Healing is not a passive process; it's an intentional journey. Intentional living becomes the compass, guiding us through self-awareness, understanding, and a departure from the victim mentality. It's a commitment to being present and giving back to the well-being of our experiences.

The unpredictable guides:

Life's journey is studded with guides, some expected, others surprising. These guides are not always close confidants; they could be strangers whose paths intersect with ours. They are the unexpected mentors, ready to lend a hand and propel us forward. The lesson here is to be open to assistance, even from the unlikeliest sources. Trust the process and shift your mindset to recognize that you are never alone on this journey.

A triumvirate of self-empowerment: acknowledge, love, bet

Amidst life's uncertainties, a triumvirate emerges—the power of self-acknowledgment, self-love, and self-care. Acknowledge the journey, with all its intricacies and imperfections. Love yourself unconditionally, recognizing that growth often emerges from the fertile soil of self-compassion. Bet on yourself—a wager that the puzzle of life, when approached with intention, will connect into a meaningful whole.

So, as you stand at the crossroads of "What's Next?" remember that the journey is not just about understanding what happened but crafting what happens next. It's about acknowledging, loving, and betting on the incredible strength within you. Life's intricate and unpredictable puzzle aligns into a beautiful mosaic when lived intentionally and with a deep belief in one's capacity for growth.

As we delve into this chapter, I would like to offer fundamental tips to keep you moving forward:

1. **Identify your strengths:** Reflect on your strengths — the qualities and capabilities that have carried you through challenges. These are the building blocks of your resilient foundation.

2. **Acknowledge setbacks:** Embrace setbacks as stepping stones, acknowledging that they have contributed to shaping your current self.

3. **Craft a vision:** Envision the person you aspire to become. Use this vision as a guidepost for building a foundation that aligns with your goals.

Stop Hiding:

4. **Authenticity:** Embrace authenticity as your superpower. No longer feel the need to hide; let the world see the real, unfiltered you.

5. **Self-acceptance:** Practice self-acceptance. Understand that imperfections are part of the human experience and contribute to your unique story.

Open yourself to a new future:

1. **Goal setting:** Define clear and achievable goals for the future. These goals will give direction and purpose to your "Now what?" phase.
2. **Embrace change:** Cultivate an open mindset. The future is full of possibilities, and embracing change is a powerful way to navigate uncertainty.

Heal and live with intention:

1. **Seek support:** Don't hesitate to seek support on your healing journey. Whether from friends, family, or professionals, support is a valuable resource.
2. **Mindfulness practices:** Integrate mindfulness practices into your daily routine. Mindfulness fosters self-awareness and helps in the intentional living process.

Be open to unexpected guides along the journey:

1. **Be open:** Be open to unexpected mentors and guides. Wisdom often comes from the most unexpected sources.

2. **Networking:** Expand your network. Connect with diverse individuals who can provide different perspectives and insights.

Practice self-acknowledgment, self-love, self-bet:

1. **Daily affirmations:** Practice daily affirmations. Affirmations reinforce self-acknowledgment, self-love, and self-belief.
2. **Set small goals:** Break down larger goals into smaller, achievable tasks. Celebrate small victories along the way.

"Your present circumstances don't determine where you can go; they merely determine where you start."
- Nido Qubein

Separation brings appreciation

The essence of separating can be challenging and devastating to understand, but openness allows us to acknowledge that we need it. There's a lot of appreciation for separation. First, it allows you to work on yourself. Second, it removes the tendency to point fingers or assign blame. Third, it allows us to take ownership of our lives and decisions.

So, when you hear separation, how does this make you feel? Can you be open to it, understanding it can be helpful rather than sinking into a place of sadness? Acknowledge where you are and how you feel, and then take steps towards working on yourself. The good stuff lies ahead, but it requires acceptance. Take charge of what is happening to the best of your ability and create a roadmap to healing and happiness.

What are the actionable steps that we need to take? Sometimes, we may feel like there's no way to restore relationships, but separation often lets us gain clarity. Is the issue with the other person, is it the environment, or are we the problem? I remember going through my journey of separation, enduring eleven months of uncertainty. It was so confusing; I didn't understand what was going on. Being away from my kids and family for so many months due to incarceration was different due to our daily routines and engagement I never thought I would have experienced such grief. Yet, in separation, I found an opportunity to look within, allowing myself to heal and forgive myself and others. Although I questioned how I got to where I was, I found peace beyond the walls and could work on myself by tapping into my childhood and forgiving the past.

In my experience, separation truly brought me understanding. During this time, God gave me peace, and I gained a better perspective on those who I once blamed for the cost of trauma in my life. In this chapter, I want to expand your perspective, focusing on personal growth and forgiving yourself and others. Separation, though isolation for a time, can be very healthy. Through this isolation, we reconnect with our essence and live our best lives authentically. "Healing is not a destination; it's a journey of self-discovery, forgiveness, and embracing the essence of your resilience. You reclaim pieces of yourself in every step, crafting a narrative of strength and renewal." Dare to live again"

Navigating the landscape of separation:

1. **Opportunity for self-work:** Separation offers a unique opportunity for self-reflection and personal development. It's a period where the focus shifts inward, enabling individuals to embark on self-improvement and growth.

2. **Removing the blame game:** The act of separating strips away the inclination to point fingers or assign blame. It departs from the "whose fault is it" narrative, fostering a deeper understanding of the complex dynamics.

3. **Ownership and access:** Separation invites individuals to own their emotions and actions. If allowed and given access, it's a space where one can delve into self-awareness and transformative personal development.

Exploring emotional responses to separation:

1. **Acknowledgment of feelings:** The chapter prompts readers to confront their emotional responses to separation. It challenges them to be open to the experience, questioning whether it is perceived as helpful or if there's a tendency to sink into a prolonged sadness.

2. **Temporal nature of separation:** A key realization emphasized is that separation, though isolated, is not a perpetual state. Understanding that it's a transient phase opens the door to rejoicing in the present and envisioning a future beyond the current emotional landscape.

The personal journey through separation

1. **Confusion, healing, and forgiveness:** A personal narrative unfolds, recounting a journey of eleven months of separation. The confusion, the struggle to comprehend, and the emotional distance from family and routine are vividly described. However, the author found a sanctuary for self-discovery, healing, and forgiveness within this separation.

2. **Tapping into the essence:** Separation becomes a canvas for tapping into one's essence, authentically confronting the past, and forgiving both oneself and others. It's a process that goes beyond questioning how one arrived at this point to finding peace beyond the walls that confine.

Expanding perspectives:

1. **Working on oneself and forgiveness:** I want to encourage you to expand your thinking and focus on self-improvement and forgiveness. Separation is posited as a healthy, albeit isolated, phase during which one dis-

covers the essence of one's core, paving the way to living authentically.

In essence, when approached with openness and a commitment to self-work, separation becomes more than a period of isolation. It becomes a transformative journey, a corridor leading to the authentic living of one's best life. This chapter serves as a guide, challenging individuals to acknowledge, understand, and step forward in separation, finding healing and the essence of their true selves.

> *"Life is not a solo act. It's a grand ensemble where every experience and connection weaves a unique melody. Embrace the harmony of your journey, and let the notes of courage, wisdom, and joy resonate with the beauty that is your life."*
> - **Florida Scott-Maxwell**

Live again and learn from the lessons:

It is in the ordinary walk that we find beauty. Permit yourself to change course rapidly from a foundation of acceptance and support. As you commit to nurturing your relationships with yourself, it's essential to embrace life with fresh eyes. Embrace what seems complicated today and accept the challenge of learning the lessons beauty in the ordinary brings. Fall in love with the process; there will be plenty of opportunities to get discouraged, lose your passion, and think it's not meant to be for you. Be your beautiful and authentic self. Embarking on this journey is not as picturesque as some make it out to be. It requires hard work and dedication. I hope this new month brings clarity, peace, joy, and abundance. May the new month reset your mind to rejuvenate your spirit. Every day, I'm reminded that not everything requires a response and deserves our attention. Letting go of your ego is essential when trying to recreate your life. They say the key to self-love lies in how we treat ourselves and spend time with others. Looking back over my life, I appreciate where I have been and how far I've come.

Finding beauty in the ordinary walk

Life's journey unfolds as we step beyond the walls that once confined us. In this new chapter, we heed the call to live again, to learn from the lessons that life has woven into our narrative, and to find beauty in the ordinary walk. It's a journey of self-discovery, transformation, and the unwavering commitment to nurture the most important relationship—with oneself.

Living again: embrace the new view of life

1. **Permission to change course:** Give yourself liberating permission to change your course. Life is fluid, and growth often requires a shift in direction. The foundation for such changes is acceptance and the support of acknowledging one's innate capacity to redefine one's path.

2. **Commitment to self-nurturing:** Central to this chapter is the unwavering commitment to nur-

turing the relationship with oneself. Self-care is not a luxury but a necessity in the hustle and bustle of life. It involves treating oneself with kindness, embracing imperfections, and recognizing the inherent worthiness of self-love.

The challenge of embracing today:

1. **Embracing the challenging moments:** Acknowledge that life is a tapestry of easy and challenging moments. Embrace what comes hard today, for it is often in facing challenges that we unearth our most profound strengths. Each challenge is an opportunity for growth and resilience.

2. **Falling in love with the process:** "Embrace the process of transformation. It's not always adorned with butterflies and dancing but rather involves setbacks, introspection, and the resilience to keep moving forward. Find beauty in the unfolding story, regardless of the unexpected detours.".

Words of wisdom and affirmations:

1. **Navigating the journey:** In the journey of transformation, expect not just butterflies but storms. Yet, it's in navigating through storms that we find the strength to soar to new heights.

2. **Resetting the mind and rejuvenating the spirit:** May this new month bring clarity, peace, joy, and abundant increase. Let it reset your mind

and rejuvenate your spirit for the beautiful journey ahead.

Reflections on self-love:

1. **Learning the art of non-response:** Every day, I learn that everything doesn't constitute a response. Every action doesn't need my reaction. Everything doesn't require attention. Sometimes, letting things be is the most powerful response.

2. **The importance of self-love in recreating life:** They say the only way to recreate your life is when you love yourself in the way you spend time with others. In that moment of life, ego fades, and authenticity shines.

Appreciating the journey:

1. **Reflection on the past:** "As I look back over my life, I appreciate where I've been and how each step, whether easy or challenging, has brought me to this moment of growth and self-discovery."

The once-ordinary walk transforms into something truly extraordinary in rediscovering life and learning from its lessons. It's a path that demands bravery, self-compassion, and a deep appreciation for the beauty hidden in every stride. This chapter invites the reader to not only face the challenges but to embrace them, fall in love with the journey of growth, and uncover the joy within every step of self-renewal. It's a reminder that even the most minor steps forward are part of a remarkable transformation.

> "Embrace the vulnerability of your journey, for it is in ordinary, messy moments that you discover your extraordinary strength. As Brene Brown wisely reminds us, 'Vulnerability is not winning or losing; it's having the courage to show up and be seen when we have no control over the outcome."

GIVE YOURSELF TIME TO HEAL...

Grow Through What You Go Through....

Just like the butterfly, we undergo our transformational journey. Through struggles and setbacks, we emerge stronger, wiser, and ready to spread our wings and fly. The butterfly teaches us that change is inevitable, but growth is optional. Embrace the process, for within it lies the beauty of becoming.

CHAPTER 5

The Challenges of Re-entry

"In the crucible of challenges, we find our resilience and the raw materials for rebuilding. Beyond These Walls, in the heart of adversity, lies the canvas upon which we paint our story of hope and transformation."

As I share my experience and understanding of the re-entry process, its complexity becomes apparent. Re-entry and rebuilding one's life after incarceration or adversity can be a daunting and challenging task. There are many obstacles to overcome, including external and psychological impediments that may hinder progress and success. However, with the right mindset, support, and resources, these obstacles can be conquered, creating a better future. One of the biggest hurdles for those re-entering society after incarceration is finding a permanent job. Many businesses are hesitant to hire people with criminal backgrounds, making it challenging for them to provide for their families. Additionally, limited skills and education can make securing higher-paying jobs and maintaining a stable lifestyle difficult. Education and vocational training can also be beneficial, providing people with the skills and knowledge needed to secure better-paying jobs and establish a secure future. Furthermore, education and training can help increase self-esteem and confidence, providing a sense of purpose and achievement.

Rebuilding relationships with friends and family who may have been affected by the incarceration can also be challenging. Incarceration can damage relationships and create feelings of isolation, making reconnecting with loved ones difficult. Feelings of guilt and shame may further complicate this process. To navigate the challenges of re-entry successfully, adopting a positive mindset and maintaining hope for the future is essential. Seeking assistance from support groups, community organizations, and mental health professionals can provide invaluable support and guidance.

Reintegration can also be emotionally and psychologically draining. People may experience anxiety, despair, and low self-esteem as they attempt to rebuild their lives. The stigma and prejudice surrounding people with criminal records can make them feel ashamed and isolated.

Forgiveness of oneself and others plays a pivotal role in the journey of re-entry and rebuilding. It's essential to acknowledge past mistakes without allowing them to define one's future. Forgiving oneself for past transgressions allows personal growth and liberation from self-doubt and self-sabotage. Furthermore, extending forgiveness to those who may not be emotionally available to assist in the journey can be empowering. Recognizing that everyone has their own struggles and limitations can help release resentment and move forward with compassion and understanding.

It's crucial to validate one's feelings and experiences throughout reintegration. Self-sabotage can often stem from feelings of unworthiness or inadequacy. However, by acknowledging and honoring one's emotions, individuals can pave the way for self-acceptance and realizing the opportunities that await them. While the road to reintegration may be fraught with challenges, it is also brimming with opportunities for growth and transformation. By embracing forgiveness, self-validation, and resilience, individuals can navigate the journey with courage and determination, ultimately finding the light beyond the walls of adversity.

Transforming Challenges into Opportunities for Hopeful Futures

"In the delicate art of rebuilding connections, warmth is the glue that binds wounds, and hope is the compass guiding us forward. As we navigate the reintegration terrain, the returning individual and their loved ones carry the weight of past pain. Yet, in this shared journey, there's an opportunity to co-create a future filled with understanding, forgiveness, and a renewed sense of belonging. Patience becomes a tool, understanding a skill, and love the foundation upon which trust is rebuilt. With open hearts and the right support, we can weave a tapestry of connection that withstands the tests of time."

The emotional toll of re-entry and the importance of mental health and substance abuse support.

Reentry into society after confinement can be a challenging experience that can take a significant emotional toll on individuals. Therefore, it is crucial to prioritize mental health and substance abuse support during this time. Individuals may violate their probation without proper care or guidance and return to confinement. Providing help and support to improve their well-being and setting up a plan to reach their optimal health while in treatment can aid in the healing and restoration of the individual. Here are some options to consider.

Navigating re-entry and building a supportive community with hope for individuals leaving incarceration involves a comprehensive approach that addresses mental health and substance abuse support. Here are some strategies to consider:

Accessible Mental Health Services:

- Ensure individuals can access mental health services, including counseling and therapy. Collaborate with mental health professionals and organizations to provide support tailored to the unique needs of those re-entering society.

Substance Abuse Treatment Programs:

- Develop and promote accessible substance abuse treatment programs. Offering counseling, support groups, and rehabilitation services can be critical in addressing addiction issues and preventing relapse.

Community-Based Support Groups:

- Establish community-based support groups where individuals can share their experiences, challenges, and successes. Peer support is invaluable in fostering a sense of belonging and understanding.

Employment Assistance:

- Work with local businesses and organizations to create employment opportunities for individuals with a history of incarceration. Job training programs and partnerships with employers willing to give second chances can enhance re-entry success.

Education and Skill Building:

- Provide educational opportunities and skill-building programs to empower individuals and provide them with the tools needed for personal and professional growth. This can include vocational training, literacy programs, and educational resources.

Housing stability:

Address housing instability by collaborating with housing authorities, landlords, and non-profits to secure safe and stable housing options for individuals re-entering the community. Stable housing is a fundamental factor in reducing recidivism.

Legal assistance:

- Offer legal assistance and resources to help individuals navigate legal challenges post-release. This includes addressing issues related to employment, housing, and family reunification.

Family reintegration support:

- Recognize the importance of family reunification and provide support services to facilitate healthy relationships. Family-focused counseling, parenting programs, and communication support can strengthen family bonds.

Community Education and Awareness:

- Conduct community education programs to dispel myths and reduce the stigma surrounding individuals with a criminal history. Fostering understanding and empathy can contribute to creating a more supportive environment.

Crisis Intervention Plans:

- Develop crisis intervention plans that address potential setbacks, relapses, or emergencies. A well-defined support system can prevent individuals from falling through the cracks during challenging times.

Collaboration with Faith-Based Organizations:

- Engage with faith-based organizations that may provide additional support, mentorship, and community resources. Many faith communities are committed to helping individuals rebuild their lives.

Building a community with hope requires ongoing collaboration between government agencies, non-profits, businesses, and the community. By addressing mental health, substance abuse, and various re-entry challenges collectively, it becomes possible to create a more inclusive and supportive environment for individuals seeking to reintegrate into society.

CHAPTER 6

Embracing Inner Healing and Renewal

"Discover the inner healing and renewal journey as you lead your own life. In the depths of self-discovery, find the courage to release the past, cultivate inner strength, and step boldly into the future, empowered to create the life you envision. The power lies within you."

Clean out the basement, yes, clean out the basement, that's what I heard. I looked around the room, trying to figure out what that voice meant and where it came from. In our journey towards self-discovery and healing, we must embark on cleaning out the basement of our lives. This metaphorical journey involves letting go of the emotional clutter and baggage that may have accumulated over time, allowing us to create space for new beginnings and inner transformation. When we are dealing with difficulties in life and just recovering from mishaps or decisions we have made, there's still clutter in our souls, noise in our minds, and something blocking our ability to take steps forward.

I can share a little story about what I kept in my basement. I kept a lot of childhood trauma, which affected my behavioral style and how I was communicating and engaging with myself and others. I was very defensive, reactive, and self-centered. I wasn't kind to myself or compassionate when I made mistakes. At times, I found myself engulfed in negative self-talk due to the wounds I inflicted upon others or my error and their interpretations of my actions. It's during moments of pain, hurt, or transitions, whether as an adolescent, a young adult, or a new parent, that we often overlook the profound growth inherent in these experiences. We don't understand how to treat ourselves without exposure to healthy self-care practices. If the environment that one lives in is not nurturing, it can be detrimental to our well-being.

I say clean out your metaphorical basement by forgiving those who unknowingly hurt you because they were hurt themselves. It's about cultivating a supportive environment conducive to personal growth, ensuring that past struggles don't seep into the promises of our future.. Beneath the surface of our conscious awareness lies a basement filled with old beliefs, unresolved emotions, and forgotten dreams. In "Clearing out the basement," we embark on self-discovery and transformation, clearing the clutter to create space for the life we deserve. By confronting the shadows of our past and releasing what no longer serves us, we pave the way for growth, fulfillment, and authenticity.

Acknowledging the Clutter: Our basement is a repository of cherished and painful memories. It holds outdated beliefs, fears, and insecurities that weigh us down and prevent us from reaching our full potential. Acknowledging the clutter, we take the first step towards reclaiming our power and creating a life aligned with our deepest desires.

Letting Go of the Past: To live the life we deserve, we must free ourselves from the grip of the past. This entails letting go of regrets, resentments, and self-limiting beliefs that anchor us to old patterns and prevent us from moving forward. Through forgiveness, acceptance, and self-love, we free ourselves from yesterday's shackles and open ourselves to new possibilities.

Creating Space for Growth: As we clear out the debris of the past, we create space for growth, creativity, and abundance. We cultivate an environment that nurtures our dreams and aspirations, surrounding ourselves with positivity, inspiration, and support. By decluttering our physical space, we declutter our minds, allowing clarity and purpose to emerge.

Embracing Authenticity: Living the life we deserve requires authenticity and alignment with our true selves. We embrace our quirks, imperfections, and unique gifts, celebrating the essence of who we are. By honoring our authenticity, we attract opportunities and relationships that resonate with our soul, leading to greater fulfillment and joy.

Stepping into Your Power: As we clear out the basement, we reclaim our power and take ownership of our lives. We make empowered choices, set boundaries, and pursue our passions with courage and conviction. By stepping into our power, we create the life we deserve—one filled with purpose, meaning, and abundance.

Action Steps:

1. Start Small: Begin by tackling one area of your basement at a time, whether physical or emotional clutter.
2. Reflect and Release: Reflect on what no longer serves you and consciously release it with gratitude and forgiveness.
3. Surround Yourself with Support: Seek out a supportive community or enlist the help of friends and family to assist you in your journey.
4. Cultivate Self-Compassion: Be gentle with yourself throughout the process, recognizing that change takes time and effort.
5. Celebrate Progress: Acknowledge each step forward, no matter how small, and celebrate the victories.

Conclusion: In "Cleaning out the basement," we embark on a journey of liberation and self-discovery, shedding the past's layers to reveal our true selves' brilliance. By confronting the clutter, letting go of what no longer serves us, and embracing authenticity, we create the space for a life filled with purpose, passion, and possibility. Let us clear out the basement and step into the abundant life we deserve.

> *"Breaking free from the confines of our past, we clear the clutter of yesterday's shadows to unveil the boundless potential that awaits us beyond these walls."*

What do you have to let go of? Embracing Freedom and Resilience Beyond the Walls

> **Quote for Resilience:** *"In the depths of adversity lies the opportunity to discover the resilience that resides within us, guiding us to rise above our challenges and thrive."*

Every day, I remind myself that I have been given another chance. But with each passing year, I realize there are things I must let go of to walk in the light of life. I've questioned myself, wondering what keeps me from shining brightly. Well, here we go; the truth is, even though I was physically released from prison in 2008, I kept myself imprisoned in so many areas of my life as it became a mindset for me. Shame played a big role in my life, as I worried about what others might think or say about me.

It is important to recognize that we will encounter mishaps and setbacks in life, and none of them can determine where God will take us. It's always our inner critic, fueled by the opinions of others, that keeps us trapped in shame. For the past 17 years since my release, I've struggled with this. In this chapter, I want you to know that I am writing, expressing, and sharing because when I say no one is exempt from experiencing a drastic shift in their lives, we will encounter challenges. It is about how we see it and embracing the shifts shaping our journey.

I've had to let go of the thoughts that haunted me, preventing me from fully embracing and loving myself. From the traumas of my childhood to the unhealthy patterns I carried into adulthood, I've had to confront my past to move forward. And I've realized that many of us suffer in silence because we lack the space to express our pain due to judgment.

Letting go is so important. It allows you to be free internally, emotionally, and physically, knowing that someday, you can share your side of the story from a place of joy, inspiring others to live without shame by releasing their burdens. My journey began with my noisy childhood, where I learned harmful behaviors that followed me into adulthood. But now, I'm breaking free from those chains, no longer controlled by the need to please others.

In life's journey, we often find ourselves held back by the weight of our past experiences and the shadows that linger within us. In "letting go," we confront the barriers that imprison our hearts and minds, discovering the transformative power of releasing what no longer serves us. Through resilience, self-discovery, and acceptance, we embark on a journey of healing and liberation, unlocking the doors to a brighter, more authentic existence.

Tips and Motivation:

1. Embrace Self-Reflection: Take time to look inward and identify the thoughts, beliefs, and behaviors that hold you back. Self-awareness is the first step towards liberation.

2. Practice Forgiveness: Release resentment and grudges toward yourself and others. Forgiveness does not condone actions but frees you from the burden of carrying them.

3. Cultivate Self-Compassion: Treat yourself with kindness and understanding, acknowledging that you are worthy of love and acceptance.

4. Seek Support: Contact trusted friends, family members, or professionals who can offer guidance, encouragement, and perspective on your journey.

5. Challenge Limiting Beliefs: Question the validity of negative thoughts and beliefs that keep you trapped in shame and self-doubt. Replace them with affirming and empowering truths.

6. Engage in Healing Practices: Explore therapeutic modalities such as journaling, mindfulness, or expressive arts to process and release emotional wounds.

7. Set Boundaries: Establish healthy boundaries to protect your well-being and honor your needs and values. Learn to say no to activities or relationships that drain your energy or compromise your integrity.

8. Practice Gratitude: Cultivate a mindset of gratitude, focusing on the blessings and opportunities surrounding you. Gratitude shifts your perspective from lack to abundance.

9. Embrace Imperfection: Let go of the need for perfection and embrace the beauty of your flaws and vulnerabilities. Imperfection is what makes you uniquely human.

10. Celebrate Progress: Acknowledge and celebrate the steps you take towards letting go and reclaiming your freedom. Every small victory is a testament to your resilience and strength.

Conclusion: In letting go to start embracing the freedom given to us," we confront the chains that bind us, freeing ourselves from the prisons of our own making. Through resilience, courage, and self-compassion, we release the burdens of the past and step into a future filled with possibility and joy. As we embark on this journey of liberation, may we find solace in knowing that we are not alone and that by letting go, we embrace the freedom to live authentically and entirely beyond the walls that once confined us?

> *"True freedom is found in the courage to let go of what holds you back and embrace the limitless possibilities that await you."*
> - **Tony Robbins.**

Life is a unique journey for each of us. Let's make the most of it

However, grasping this understanding was a significant challenge as I navigated beyond the walls I created. Returning home to society was a journey of its own, one without a set path for re-entry. Reclaiming my life again took so long because I felt like all doors were closed. Despite having my own business, I still carried a heavy burden of guilt for letting down my children, my mother, and those around me. This self-imposed narrative of failure kept me trapped in my mental prison long after my physical release.. The journey to reclaim life felt extraordinary due to seemingly insurmountable obstacles. Just learn, be patient with yourself, celebrate progress, and keep moving forward.

While many of us may benefit from formal therapy, we might gain the perspective or support we need if we take the time to understand ourselves and process our emotions through journaling or conversations with loved ones. I have found solace in revisiting memories from my childhood. It's important to recognize that different children react differently to pain; some may try to hide it, while others may express it more openly.

I firmly believe that while formal therapy can be beneficial for many, we often underestimate the power of introspection, journaling, and meaningful conversations with loved ones. I've found solace in revisiting my childhood experiences, recognizing that our early years shape many aspects of our adult lives. Just as I've witnessed the varied reactions of my children to pain, I've come to understand that we all have different ways of processing emotions and experiences. Some may bottle up their feelings, while others express them dramatically. Regardless, the key is acknowledging and accepting these emotions rather than suppressing them.

Acknowledging our feelings, whether sadness, anger, or fear, is essential for our emotional well-being. I recognize myself as someone who feels deeply and experiences strong emotions. After years of suppressing this, I've instead learned to allow myself to feel deeply while maintaining control. This journey of self-discovery has been ongoing, but it has empowered me to embrace authenticity and vulnerability as strengths rather than weaknesses.

Standing at the crossroads of "Now what?" let us remember that the journey is not just about understanding what happened. It's about crafting what happens next. When we live intentionally and with a deep belief in our capacity for growth, we can transform life's intricate and unpredictable puzzle into a beautiful mosaic.

This chapter offers the following basic tips to keep you moving forward: First, reflect on your strengths—the qualities and capabilities that have carried you through challenges. These are the building blocks of your resilient foundation. Second, embrace setbacks as stepping stones, acknowledging that they have contributed to the person you are today. Third, envision the person you aspire to become, using this vision as a guidepost for building a foundation that aligns with your goals. No longer hide behind a mask of perfection. Embrace authenticity as your superpower. Understand that imperfections are part of the human experience and contribute to your unique story. Practice self-acceptance and let the world see the real, unfiltered you.

Define clear and achievable goals for the future. These goals will give direction and purpose to your "Now what?" phase. Cultivate a mindset that is open to change. The future is full of possibilities, and embracing change is a powerful way to navigate uncertainty.

Don't hesitate to seek support on your healing journey. Support is a valuable resource, whether it comes from friends, family, or professionals.

Integrate mindfulness practices into your daily routine. Mindfulness fosters self-awareness and helps in the intentional living process.

Be open to unexpected mentors and guides. Wisdom often comes from the most unexpected sources. Expand your network. Connect with diverse individuals who can provide different perspectives and insights. Practice daily affirmations. Affirmations reinforce self-acknowledgment, self-love, and self-belief. Break down larger goals into smaller, achievable tasks. Celebrate small victories along the way.

Separation can be hard to understand, but openness lets us know we need it. There is a positive side we can learn to appreciate. Separation allows you to work on yourself and learn to stop pointing fingers and blaming others. In this way, separation is healthy. Although it can isolate you for a while, it is often in isolation that you find authenticity, reclaiming pieces of yourself and crafting a new narrative.

Reflect on your strengths, embrace setbacks as stepping stones, and envision the person you aspire to become. Embrace authenticity, self-acceptance, and openness to change. Seek support, integrate mindfulness practices, and be open to unexpected mentors and guides.

By embracing our unique paths, listening to our inner wisdom, and cultivating practices that nurture our well-being, we enrich our lives and contribute to humanity's collective tapestry. So, as you embark on your journey, remember to savor every moment. Life is indeed different for us all, and your journey is yours to live, cherish, and celebrate.

TIME TO REFLECT AND JOURNAL...

What past pains or setbacks have significantly impacted my life?

_____
_____
_____
_____
_____
_____
_____
_____
_____

How have these experiences shaped my current beliefs and behaviors?

_____
_____
_____
_____
_____
_____
_____
_____

What steps can I take to begin healing from past traumas?

_____
_____
_____
_____
_____
_____
_____
_____

How can I rewrite my story to create a more positive narrative for my future?

_____
_____
_____
_____
_____
_____
_____
_____

What support systems can I engage with to aid my healing journey?

_____
_____
_____
_____
_____
_____
_____
_____

What emotions surface when I reflect on my experiences beyond these walls?

_____
_____
_____
_____
_____
_____
_____
_____
_____

In what ways have I been feeling stuck or hindered by traumatic life shifts?

_____
_____
_____
_____
_____
_____
_____
_____
_____

What negative thoughts or beliefs have been holding me back from my well-being?

_____
_____
_____
_____
_____
_____
_____
_____
_____

How can I reframe these negative thoughts into more positive and empowering ones?

What practices can I incorporate into my daily routine to manage my well-being effectively?

What steps can I take to cultivate self-esteem and self-acceptance in my life?

In what ways can I let go of guilt and shame and embrace self-forgiveness and compassion?

How can I strengthen my relationships with others and foster deeper connections?

A healthy mind is vital for a happy life. Therefore, it is important to look after our emotional well-being. Here are some effective "Tips for Staying Emotionally Healthy" to help you stay positive and happy.

"Every journey begins with a single step. Embrace each step forward, for they lead you closer to a brighter tomorrow."

1. It's important to remember to be patient with yourself, as healing takes time. You're doing your best, and that's all that matters.
2. Practicing gratitude daily can help shift your focus from past pain to present blessings. Take time to appreciate the good things in your life, no matter how small they may seem.
3. Feeling and expressing your emotions without judging yourself is okay. Your feelings are valid, and you deserve to be heard and understood.
4. Surrounding yourself with positivity and limiting exposure to triggers can help you create a safe and supportive environment for yourself.
5. Remember that every step forward is progress, no matter how small it may seem. Keep moving forward, and don't be too hard on yourself.
6. Identifying and prioritizing self-care practices

can help you care for yourself physically, emotionally, and mentally. Remember to be kind to yourself and make self-care a priority.

7. Setting achievable personal growth and development goals can help you stay motivated and inspired. Don't be afraid to dream big and take small steps towards achieving your goals.

8. Building a solid support network of friends, family, or community resources can help you feel connected and supported during difficult times.

9. Seeking professional help is a sign of strength, not weakness. Don't be afraid to reach out for help if you need it.

10. Practicing forgiveness towards yourself and others can help you let go of past hurts and move forward with grace and compassion.

11. Practicing self-compassion and acknowledging your progress, no matter how small, can help you build self-esteem and confidence.

12. Regular self-care activities such as exercise, meditation, and spending time outdoors can help you feel rejuvenated and refreshed.

13. Exploring therapy or counseling options to address deep-rooted hurts and traumas can be a decisive step toward healing and growth.

14. Setting realistic personal and professional development goals and celebrating achievements can help you stay motivated and inspired. Remember to honor yourself and all that you've accomplished.

Discover the power to transform negative thoughts into positive ones, nurture your well-being, embrace your self-worth, and let go of guilt and shame. Strengthen your relationships, practice mindfulness, and cultivate gratitude through daily practice. Remember, small steps can lead to big changes.

Transforming Negative Thoughts:

1. Identify recurring negative thoughts and challenge their validity.
2. Replace negative self-talk with affirmations and positive statements.
3. Practice gratitude and focus on the positives in your life.
4. Reframe obstacles as opportunities for growth and learning.

Managing Well-being:

1. Prioritize self-care routines, including adequate relaxation.
2. Develop coping strategies for managing stress and anxiety, such as deep breathing or meditation.

3. Seek professional help if needed, such as therapy or counseling.
4. Engage in activities that bring you joy and fulfillment, even in small doses.

Growing Self-esteem & Self-acceptance:

1. Practice self-compassion and treat yourself with kindness.
2. Celebrate your accomplishments and acknowledge your strengths.
3. Challenge perfectionistic tendencies and embrace your imperfections.
4. Surround yourself with supportive and uplifting people.

Letting Go of Guilt and Shame:

1. Recognize that everyone makes mistakes and forgive yourself.
2. Focus on lessons learned from past experiences rather than dwelling on regrets.
3. Practice self-compassion and remind yourself that you deserve forgiveness.
4. Engage in activities that promote self-forgiveness and healing.

Strengthening Relationships:

1. Communicate openly and honestly with loved ones.

2. Practice active listening and empathy in your interactions.
3. Spend quality time together and create shared experiences.
4. Express appreciation and gratitude for the people in your life.

Tips for Mindfulness:

1. Practice mindfulness meditation to ground yourself in the present moment.
2. Engage in mindful activities such as walking, eating, or breathing exercises.
3. Cultivate awareness of your thoughts and emotions without judgment.
4. Incorporate mindfulness into daily routines, such as mindful eating or communication. Add Yoga to your life and give yourself the gift of stillness.

Creating a Gratitude List:

Creating a gratitude list is a wonderful practice that can positively affect our well-being. Here are five health benefits of maintaining a gratitude list:

1. Gaining perspective: Life can be challenging, and sometimes we feel drained and overwhelmed. However, a gratitude list helps us see beyond challenges. Even during difficult moments, there are things to be grateful for.

This tool helps us prevent our minds from being clouded by negativity and reminds us of the positive aspects of life.

2. Enhancing self-reflection and orientation: By regularly creating gratitude lists, we become aware of what we truly appreciate. Often, our desires differ from what we genuinely value. For instance, while we may dream of wealth or success, our gratitude list might reveal that we crave rest and balance. It helps us understand ourselves better and align our priorities.

3. Fostering hope: When our mental health deteriorates, hope can fade away. A gratitude list serves as a beacon of hope. It reminds us that there are reasons to keep going even in challenging times. It's a gentle nudge toward optimism and resilience.

4. Stress reduction: Our minds are powerful, and practicing gratitude can significantly reduce stress. Focusing on what we're thankful for shifts our attention away from stressors. It's like a mental reset button that calms our nerves and promotes emotional well-being.

5. Enhancing relationships: Gratitude fosters deeper connections with others. Expressing appreciation strengthens our bonds. Whether acknowledging a friend's kindness or appreciating a family member's support, gratitude en-

riches our relationships and brings joy to both the giver and the receiver.

Remember, your gratitude list doesn't need to be elaborate—simple moments, gestures, and blessings count. Start jotting down what you are thankful for, and watch how it positively impacts your life!

A Note to You, My Dear Friend

I hope this message finds you at peace, no matter where you are today. I want to take a moment to remind you of something simple yet profoundly powerful: the importance of healing and finding stillness during life's chaos.

Life may sometimes feel overwhelming, but remember, you don't have to rush through your healing. Take time to pause, breathe, and allow yourself the space to feel. One practice that can help you on this journey is maintaining a gratitude list. I know things might be difficult right now, but reflecting on even the smallest blessings can tremendously impact your heart and mind.

A gratitude list doesn't need to be extravagant. It's about acknowledging the little things—the smile of a loved one, the warmth of the sun, or the comfort of a quiet moment. Shifting your focus toward these small joys can create a ripple of peace, even when the world feels heavy. It helps you gain perspective, reminding you about the good things in your life.

As you continue this journey, I encourage you to be gentle with yourself. Forgive yourself for the moments when you feel like you're not moving fast enough or when things don't go as planned. Healing is not a race. Be kind to your spirit and remember that self-forgiveness is as important as forgiving others.

You deserve joy, peace, and renewal. By embracing stillness, practicing gratitude, and offering compassion, you can invite more healing into your life, one step at a time.

I'm rooting for you. Always.

With love and compassion,

Your Motivator

CHAPTER 7

Despite the detours, I am ready to take on another live event with renewed determination

---

"Are you looking to overcome tragedy and live again? It all starts with creating a safe space to talk about your experiences. By sharing your story, you're taking the first step towards resilience, integrity, understanding, purpose, and hope. These are the essential ingredients to becoming the best version of yourself, especially after setbacks such as divorce, loss, or imprisonment. Don't let your hardships define you; let them inspire you to grow and evolve. Remember, prison is not just a physical place; it's also a state of mind. By being motivated to overcome obstacles and staying hopeful, you can break free from the mental confines that hold you back. So, let's come together to share our stories and inspire others to keep moving forward. You got this!"

Breaking Free: Embracing Resilience and Hope

As we start to embrace resilience, it becomes apparent that acceptance is a key component. Acceptance involves acknowledging the events that have occurred and our role in them. It's about recognizing how we may have allowed ourselves to be in situations of pain or hurt or how we've internalized the negative perceptions others have cast upon us. For many of us, bouncing back from adversity isn't instinctual. It's a skill that must be nurtured and developed through healthy coping mechanisms. In my journey, I've found solace in providing hope to those around me, even amidst my struggles.

Returning home from incarceration was so daunting, an experience shrouded in shame and stagnation. Yet, understanding resilience has been enlightening. Resilience isn't just about enduring or quickly recovering from difficulties; it's about the elasticity of the human spirit and the capacity to rebound and reshape us after hardship. However, even after my physical release from confinement, I found myself imprisoned by my mindset.

Building back isn't just about reclaiming lost ground; it's about self-discovery and growth. It's about understanding the depths of our pain and seeking support from those who uplift us.

In creating this book, I aim to show readers that life's challenges are inevitable. Whether it's divorce, being a young parent, academic setbacks, career hurdles, or losing your home, we will face difficulties. Yet the beauty lies in what we learn from these challenges and how we build back. Building back is about learning who you are and what you've grown out of, understanding the pain, how it is affecting your healing process, and seeking support. It's also about confronting our narratives and taking responsibility for our choices, even amidst mental health struggles.

I want to address a crucial aspect of my journey without diminishing the responsibility I hold for the choices I make. It's important to mention that while I was grappling with mental health challenges, mainly depression, diagnosed in 2002, it wasn't readily apparent to those around me. Despite my inner struggles, outwardly, I was often perceived as joyful and lively— they did not know the turmoil I was experiencing internally.

Many close to me may have harbored judgments, but I never confronted or defended myself against their perceptions. Perhaps I internalized a belief that I was alone in facing such problems, as everyone else appeared to navigate life effortlessly. However, reflecting on it now, I recognize that vulnerability and open communication were lacking, both on my part and theirs.

It is crucial to understand that differing perspectives shape our understanding of the world. What one person perceives may not necessarily align with another's reality. In hindsight, I realize that my constant busyness and avoidance of introspection served as a means of escapism—a frantic attempt to outrun my thoughts and emotions. Growing up, I was often judged for my boundless energy and constant activity. But in truth, I was merely evading the deeper issues I was experiencing as a young adult and mother that were plaguing my mind and soul.

As I write this chapter in late 2022, I must admit that writing has proven difficult, largely due to the weight of others' opinions that I've allowed to influence me. It's a common pitfall—we often let the judgments of others seep into our self-perception, preventing us from expressing ourselves authentically. Despite the hurdles, I've come to a profound realization: I know who I am and what I stand for in this chapter of my life. It's now October 2022, and I had planned to complete this book by 2018. However, the journey has been prolonged by my insecurities and the self-doubt consequence of worrying about the judgment others will cast on me, considering my past experiences, including incarceration and separation.

Reflecting on my aggressive nature, I've come to understand that it's not merely about challenging others but confronting the inner demons that hold me back. There's a fine line between assertiveness and people-pleasing, and I've often straddled it. Yet, I've made strides in shedding the need to please everyone instead of focusing on what aligns with my values and purpose. I aim to share my story with others, helping them see their true beauty.

This is precisely why I had to finish this book, even though it's taken me a little longer than expected. I'll admit that part of the delay stemmed from my desire for perfection, for the words to sound just right. But amidst this struggle, I have felt the grace of God guiding me and surrounding me with supportive individuals.

These are not just friends from my past; they're companions on a deeper level who understand that our connection goes beyond mere history.

Reflecting on 2022, I realize that, since 2019, I've been on a transformative journey where God has stripped away the unnecessary clutter and allowed me to walk authentically in my truth. It is a journey of sharing hope with others, being unapologetically myself, and overcoming the tendency to dim my light in response to external opinions.

In life, there are moments when we stumble and allow others' judgments to overshadow our true selves. However, I have understood that authenticity is non-negotiable, especially when sharing one's story. In doing so, I've learned the importance of filling my cup first, of being in a place of overflow to nurture and support those around me.

This book isn't just for individuals who have experienced incarceration firsthand; it's for anyone grappling with this mindset. Even after my release in 2008, I found myself trapped in a cycle of hiding and self-restriction. But now, as I share my journey openly, I realize that nothing we experience is wasted. Every trial and every setback has the potential to shape us into who we are meant to be. And today, I stand before you, not as a prisoner of my past, but as a beacon of hope and resilience for those who may be walking a similar path.

I've realized that living for myself hasn't been as challenging as I once thought, especially since my separation in 2015. I struggled to ask for help, believing I had to navigate life's challenges alone. These self-imposed narratives kept replaying in my mind, reinforcing the fact that I was solely responsible for carrying the load.

But over time, I've learned a valuable lesson: you don't have to journey through life alone. Despite mishaps, setbacks, and the inevitable ups and downs, there's an inner resilience within each of us. This resilience draws from the well of positive memories, outweighing the darkness of difficult days. Yes, there have been failures along the way, but I've come to view them not as setbacks but as opportunities for growth and learning. Every stumble becomes a chance to rise again, more robust and wiser than before.

So, I implore you to get to know, love, and trust yourself wholeheartedly. Believe that you possess the strength to overcome any obstacle and emerge as the best version of yourself. Grant yourself the freedom to live authentically and shine brightly as a beacon of light for your community, your loved ones, and those life has entrusted to your care.

Within you resides a warrior, a fighter, capable of weathering any storm. But even warriors need moments of rest and rejuvenation. Step boldly into your true self, sharing your journey with others and offering hope to those struggling. Embrace resilience as your ally, understanding that acceptance—of both past events and our role in them—is essential for growth. It's about reclaiming our power and refusing to be defined by the negative perceptions of others. And through this acceptance, we find healing for ourselves and become beacons of hope for those around us.

There is Triumph After Tragedy

It can be difficult to imagine a path forward in the face of life's most devastating blows. Yet, buried within the depths of tragedy lies the potential for triumph. This chapter is a testament to the resilience of the human spirit and the power of perseverance in the wake of adversity.

Triumph after tragedy is not just about overcoming obstacles but transcending them and emerging from the darkness with newfound strength and purpose. It's about turning pain into power, sorrow into resilience, and despair into hope.

You do not, should not, and cannot suffer in silence, not when hope exists or when there are people willing to lend a helping hand. I understand that it's not easy; I've been trapped in it myself. But the reality is, when emerging from a place of devastation, where our harshest critics often reside within us, triumph is not just possible; it's inevitable.

Throughout history, countless individuals have risen from the ashes of tragedy to achieve remarkable feats. Their stories serve as beacons of inspiration, reminding us that even in our darkest moments, there is light to be found.

In this chapter, we'll embark on a transformative journey from tragedy to triumph, drawing upon the wisdom of those who have walked this path before us. We'll uncover the lessons learned, the challenges overcome, and the victories celebrated. Through tales of resilience, courage, and perseverance, we'll discover that no tragedy is impossible, and no setback is permanent. Each obstacle we encounter is an opportunity for growth, a chance to rewrite our story and emerge stronger than before.

So, let us embark on this journey together as we uncover the triumphs that await on the other side of tragedy.

"In the depths of despair, we discover the strength to rise. In the face of adversity, we find the courage to thrive. And in the embrace of hope, we ignite the light within us, shining brightly for all to see."

Doubt is the enemy of hope

Doubt will always come, it will chase you, but that doesn't mean we should stop living, stop trying again, stop hoping, and stop believing. If your current situation looks dark and you can't see the light at the end of the tunnel, you must trust and believe there is one. Find a quiet space no matter how hectic your life may be and give yourself time to be still. Stillness is everything; the absence of movement can bring us peace and allow us to dispel the doubts that threaten to overwhelm us.

For those who are spiritual, drawing upon faith and scripture can help us to connect with our inner selves and with a higher power, reminding us that we are not alone in our struggles, that we have community. Ultimately, it is important to recognize that we possess a soul—an essence within us that remains unscathed by life's trials and tribulations. No matter the setbacks we face or the challenges that lie ahead, we are not alone.

The essence within you, your soul, your spirit, is still there, nudging at you, wanting you to talk to it and feed it with love, understanding, and support. One way to feed it is to talk to someone whom you trust about your experiences, thoughts, and feelings. Furthermore, seeking knowledge about yourself through prayer, music, outdoor meditation, yoga, and exercise can be immensely beneficial.

Consider incorporating journaling into your routine. Journaling provides a safe space to find quiet and allow what is no longer helping to come out. By journaling regularly, you can cultivate a sense of stability, happiness, and positivity within yourself. Remember, doubt may overshadow your journey, but it is not invincible. With perseverance and self-awareness, you can overcome doubt and emerge stronger. Trust in the light that resides within you—the light that can illuminate not only your path but also the paths of those around you. Embrace the journey of self-discovery, and let your soul shine brightly with love, compassion, and wisdom.

If doubt is holding us back, we must remember that it's our enemy. We must keep pushing through, putting one foot in front of the other, knowing that we will become stronger on the other side. Our journey is a place for growth, forgiveness, and learning, and it's just temporary. We must keep our heads up and keep going. We've got this.

Amidst the chaos and uncertainty, it's essential to cultivate a mindset of resilience and hope. Even when doubts creep in, we must believe that brighter days are ahead. Every challenge we face is an opportunity for growth and transformation. By embracing our inner strength and refusing to succumb to doubt, we pave the way for a brighter future filled with joy and possibility.

As we navigate the twists and turns of life's journey, let us remember these words of encouragement:

> **"Hope is the anchor that keeps us steady amidst the storms of life. It whispers to us in moments of doubt, reminding us that brighter days are on the horizon. With hope as our guide, we can navigate even the darkest nights and emerge stronger, wiser, and more resilient than ever."**

Be Free
Live Again

Embrace Freedom; you are not alone. It's time to break free from the chains that bind you. Whatever struggles you're facing, know that they no longer define you. Tear down the walls of isolation and reach out for support, for there are people who care and are ready to walk alongside you. There's always hope for a brighter tomorrow.

CHAPTER 8

The Invisible Bars

Unraveling the Mental Prisons: Understanding Incarceration Beyond Physical Confinement

It's crucial to embrace a fearless mindset, to live unbound by the shackles of fear that can hold us back. Often, we find ourselves in a state of premature action, rushing towards a goal or opportunity without proper preparation. Yet, it's essential to recognize that God's timing is perfect and prepares us for the journey he has set before us. God's preparation is not just about getting us ready for what lies ahead; it's also about developing us into individuals capable of fulfilling his purpose for our lives. Rushing ahead prematurely may lead to failure or missed opportunities, as we may not be adequately equipped to manage the responsibilities that come with our calling.

I think it's imperative, and this conversation serves as a platform to highlight the significance of preparation. The preparation phase is where proper development occurs. When we enter this phase, it's like enrolling in a training program; we anticipate elevating ourselves to a new level. It's important not to bypass or rush this crucial stage.

Diving prematurely can result in us being unprepared for the challenges ahead, leading to failure. On the other hand, there are times when we prematurely abandon a dream because we fail to see that it aligns with God's plan for us. Therefore, it's essential to allow God to guide us through the entire process of preparation, ensuring that we are fully equipped for the journey ahead.

I expressed something a couple of months ago with our church, emphasizing the value of our experiences. Through these experiences, we are prepared for the divine purpose God has prepared for us. "Be anxious for nothing" (Philippians 4:6-7) - these words have resonated with me. Rushing often leads us into seasons akin to Ishmael's, where we birth things that do not align with God's preferred plan. We may find ourselves living His permissive rather than His preferred will. Consider, what are your Ishmael moments? What have you birthed without God's permission out of impatience? New seasons handed to us by another human being rather than God's, can lead to Ishmael-like outcomes.

Abraham, the father of faith, grappled with immature decisions and births. Similarly, we may find ourselves stuck in a mindset of incarceration, not necessarily in a physical facility but within our minds. Yet, despite the challenges, we must not allow our past or emotions to dictate our future. We control our reactions and decisions, even amidst pain and shame. I felt imprisoned long after my physical release, for at least 17 years. I pursued education and rebuilt my business, yet shame and pain lingered, hindering my progress. It took time to realize that my experiences weren't setbacks but lessons. Rebuilding my company allowed me to receive tenfold what I had lost, highlighting the transformative power of resilience.

A New Beginning Awaits:

As I continue writing this book, I refuse to incarcerate myself in fear or shame. My past is now part of my present story, a testament to overcoming adversity. It's a journey of healing, growth, and embracing God's preferred will over my own. Through vulnerability and courage, I hope to inspire others to break free from their mental prisons and step into a brighter future.

This journey is not just about surviving but learning to thrive. It's about embracing God's will, which often leads us in unexpected yet transformative directions. I've learned that life's detours and challenges don't define us; rather, they offer us the opportunity to reshape our story, own our shifts, and walk confidently into the future we deserve.

In being vulnerable and courageous enough to share my own struggles and triumphs, I aim to spark something within you—the strength to break free from whatever mental prison may be holding you back. Whether it's fear, shame, guilt, or regret, know that these walls don't have to define you. They can be dismantled, brick by brick, with every act of self-compassion, courage, and faith.

No matter where you've been or what you've faced, a brighter future is waiting, and you have the power to step into it. Own the shifts that life throws your way, for they are shaping you into a more resilient, authentic version of yourself. Life is not about being trapped by the past; it's about realizing the freedom you hold to create your own path, to live fully, and to embrace all that is yet to come.

Breaking the Chains of Shame: Confronting the Stigma of Incarceration

Let's address something that is never talked about - the pervasive stigma around incarceration. It's not just about being physically confined; this confidence seeps into every other aspect of life, from relationships to jobs. Unfortunately, the system fails to prepare individuals for life beyond bars adequately. Upon release, many are left struggling with unresolved mental health issues without proper support systems in place. This lack of assistance perpetuates a cycle of struggle and hardship, making it difficult for former inmates to reintegrate into society. I am passionate about creating spaces to support individuals in progressing and thriving post-incarceration. I'm committed to addressing the well-being of those affected and understanding the complex emotions and experiences that drive behaviors. Whether it's addiction, workaholism, or relationship challenges, these issues stem from deep-seated pain and trauma that demand our attention.

In my upcoming podcast, Unpack that Be Free, I'm going to talk about various themes related to family dysfunctional dynamic, therapy, self-inflictions, incarceration, including the stigma, the prison experience, identity, and relationships; stigma links to what we call Olympics experience spaces so people who have been through the Criminal justice, relationships of any experience.

One crucial aspect we'll discuss is the impact of stigma on social reintegration. Former inmates often face discrimination in their quest for employment and struggle to navigate intimate relationships. The emotional toll of incarceration – self-doubt, anxiety, and insecurity – can hinder their ability to function and make healthy choices. Ultimately, my goal is to amplify the voices of marginalized individuals within the criminal justice system, providing a platform for their stories to be heard and understood. By fostering empathy and understanding, we can break down barriers and create a more inclusive and supportive society for all.

Finding Freedom: Navigating the Mental Landscape of Incarceration

After, I want to share avenues and resources for those who have experienced incarceration or periods of self-imposed incarceration due to life situations. Counseling, therapy, and support groups can serve as transformative spaces, facilitating inner liberation and growth. I created Dare 2 Lift It to help people live again and transition beyond the shame, pain, confusion, and opinions of others and societal stigma. There is no right way to live life, but a well-lived life is one in which you learn to forgive yourself for the past and allow yourself to become free of the past.

I've been asked if I am proud about going to prison. The funny thing is I don't think prison is the pivotal point in my journey. While I acknowledge the mistakes that led to incarceration, they do not define me. Instead, I find pride in overcoming adversity, in rising above challenges such as being a high school dropout, navigating the family dysfunction, and battling with severe mental health. These experiences have shaped me but do not overshadow my personal growth and redemption journey. After reflecting on my journey, I realize that while I'm not proud of the circumstances that led to my incarceration, I am proud of the progress I've made since then. I now operate a small business, teach life skills classes to younger adults, and provide personal growth and wellness. I have 19 years as an entrepreneur, which has been a significant accomplishment. However, I understand that the shame and stigma associated with incarceration can vary for everyone. Some may view it as a pivotal point in their journey, while others may see it as a continuation of a predetermined path.

I've created a community to help people understand that where you are today isn't your final destination. The only thing that we can do is learn again from those experiences so we can live a better, healthier life and understand that we decide to keep ourselves confined in our mental state. Through counseling, therapy, and community support, we can break free from the mental and emotional confines that stem from past decisions. My own experience of spending 11 months incarcerated taught me the importance of seeking help and not allowing past mistakes to define my future. Navigating life with a criminal record can be challenging, as opportunities may be limited. Many individuals are not adequately supported in addressing their mental health needs or reintegrating into society. However, it's crucial to give ourselves grace and the freedom to live again. Learning from past mistakes, seeking counsel, and loving ourselves are essential steps toward personal growth and freedom.

In this next chapter, I want to share some light around getting better and understanding what it takes to continue growing, glowing, and flowing toward our best selves. While the past may have happened, it no longer has the power to hold us back. We can positively impact our communities and future generations through personal, mental, physical, and emotional growth. By asking the right questions and addressing underlying issues, we can accurately assess and support individuals who have been through the criminal justice system. Every situation is unique, and not every crime should be handled similarly. Taking responsibility for our actions is crucial, as is providing opportunities for growth, redemption, and rehabilitation.

I stand as a testament to the power of personal transformation and the ability to rise above past mistakes. Together, we can break free from the chains of shame and incarceration, dare to lift ourselves, and live again. You can move forward, embrace your purpose, and create a legacy of resilience, growth, and impact. Be well, do well, and live again. Dare 2 Lift It — it's time.

CHAPTER 9

Dare 2 Lift It: Finding Freedom Within

As we move forward into living beyond the confines of those physical walls that once held us, let us embark on a journey of self-discovery, empowerment, and enlightenment. The path ahead may seem daunting, scattered with remnants of past mistakes, societal judgments, and internal struggles. Yet, in this terrain lies the potential for profound transformation, for finding liberation within us. This journey has taken longer than expected as I wasn't kind to my mind, and I allowed my past experiences to hold me back. But now I can utterly understand that this was all part of my journey, and these detours were part of my development. I share my story as I don't want anyone else to experience the confinement of allowing ourselves to dwell on things we can't change instead of celebrating that we were chosen to walk this path.

In March 2023, I struggled in this chapter when I got a call from my son that truly shifted everything. The illness of a loved one and personal celebrations all converged, reminding me of the complexity of life's seasons. During these times, I've learned the importance of authentic relationships—those that allow me to be myself, messy and imperfect, yet fully embraced and celebrated. It's in these connections that true friendship is found, where our mess becomes a message, and our journey is shared and celebrated.

I can't wait to celebrate the release of this book, which, while its completion has been long and challenging, I recognize that its timing is perfect. It's not about perfectionism; it's about the reader, who will ultimately find solace, inspiration, and hope within its pages. Beyond these walls is a physical escape and a mindset—a decision to release ourselves from self-imposed limitations and embrace the boundless possibilities that await us.

So, as I delved into Chapter 1, I found myself exploring the fact that there's no right way to live. However, amidst this understanding, there is a path—a way to live once we embrace our freedom. It's about celebrating and accepting our current state, recognizing our brilliance and vibrancy. I started talking to myself differently, kindly addressing the girl in the mirror. I started shedding the old tears, and there are now tears of joy because I can walk into a room and keep my head up high, knowing that I have the potential to inspire and uplift others who may have felt the weight of their walls. Each step we take towards reclaiming our lives is an act of courage, a testament to our resilience and determination. We must Dare 2 Lift the weight of shame, regret, and self-doubt that may have burdened us for far too long. Only by confronting these inner demons with compassion and understanding can we truly break free from their grip.

In our quest for healing and growth, let us not forget the importance of seeking support and guidance. Counseling, therapy, and support groups offer invaluable resources for navigating the complexities of our mental landscape. Through open dialogue and shared experiences, we can find solace in knowing that we are not alone in our struggles. But beyond seeking external assistance, we must also cultivate a sense of empowerment from within. We can rewrite our narratives to redefine ourselves beyond the labels society may have placed upon us. Our past does not define us; it merely serves as a chapter in our journey toward self-discovery.

I stand before you as living proof that it is possible to transcend the confines of our past mistakes and emerge stronger, wiser, and more resilient than ever before. My time behind bars was not the end of my story; it was a catalyst for growth and transformation.

I refuse to allow the stigma of my past to dictate my future. Instead, I embrace my journey, flaws and all, as a testament to the resilience of the human spirit. Each scar and setback serves as a reminder of the strength within us all.

So, my fellow travelers on this journey of self-discovery, I implore you to dare to lift yourselves, to rise above the limitations that once held you back. You are worthy of love, of forgiveness, of redemption. You have the power to create a life of purpose and meaning, to leave a legacy that transcends the confines of time and space. As we embark on this next chapter of our lives, let us do so with courage, grace, and an unwavering belief in our potential. For within each of us lies the spark of greatness waiting to be ignited. Let us dare to lift it and, in doing so, set ourselves free to live, to love, and to thrive once more.

> *"True healing begins when we dare to face our pain, embrace our wounds, and nurture our souls with compassion and self-love."* – **Unknown.**

Resources for Healing and Rebuilding:

1. Mental Health Support Groups: Connect with local or online support groups focusing on mental health and emotional well-being. These groups provide a safe space for sharing experiences, gaining insights, and receiving support from others who understand your journey.

2. Therapy and Counseling Services: Seek out licensed therapists or counselors who specialize in trauma, addiction recovery, or other areas relevant to your healing journey. Therapy offers a confidential and supportive environment for exploring your emotions, thoughts, and behaviors and learning coping strategies to navigate life's challenges.

Community Programs and Outreach Initiatives: Engage with community programs and outreach initiatives, providing resources and support for individuals transitioning from incarceration to society. These programs may help with housing, employment, education, and other essential needs, helping you rebuild your life and establish a sense of stability.

1. Self-Care Practices: Incorporate self-care practices into your daily routine to nurture your physical, mental, and emotional well-being. This may include meditation, mindfulness, exercise, journaling, creative expression, and spending time in nature.

2. Education and Skill-Building: Invest in personal and professional development by pursuing education and skill-building opportunities. This could involve enrolling in courses, workshops, or vocational training programs that align with your interests and goals, empowering you to enhance your knowledge and expertise.

3. Peer Support Networks: Connect with peers who share similar experiences and goals, whether through online forums, social media groups, or community organizations. Peer support networks offer encouragement, validation, and practical advice from individuals who have walked a similar path and can provide valuable insights and perspectives.

4. Volunteer Work and Giving Back: Consider giving back to your community through volunteer work or community service projects.

Engaging in acts of kindness and altruism can foster a sense of purpose, belonging, and connection while also making a positive impact on the lives of others.

Remember that healing is a journey, and seeking support and guidance along the way is okay. By embracing these resources and committing to your personal growth and well-being, you can rebuild your life with resilience, strength, and hope.

"Freedom is not merely the absence of confinement, but the soul's liberation from the shackles of fear, doubt, and self-limiting beliefs. It is the ultimate expression of our inherent power to create our destiny."
- **Unknown**

Resilience Against External Influences:

1. Cultivate Inner Strength: Develop a strong sense of self-worth and self-confidence that is independent of external validation. Recognize your inherent value and worthiness, regardless of others' opinions or societal norms.

2. Stay Focused on Your Goals: Maintain clarity and focus on your personal and professional goals, prioritizing what is important to you over the expectations or judgments of others.

Keep your vision of freedom and success present as you navigate your path.

3. Embrace Individuality: Celebrate your unique qualities, talents, and perspectives, and resist the urge to conform to societal norms or expectations. Embrace authenticity and self-expression, allowing yourself to shine brightly in your own way.

4. Set Boundaries: Establish clear boundaries. Learn to say no to people or situations that do not align with your values or hinder your path to freedom and personal growth.

5. Seek Supportive Relationships: Surround yourself with supportive and empowering individuals who uplift and encourage you on your journey. Build a network of mentors, friends, and allies who believe in your potential and support your aspirations.

6. Practice Emotional Intelligence: Develop emotional intelligence skills to navigate challenging situations and relationships with grace and resilience. Cultivate self-awareness, self-regulation, empathy, and effective communication to manage conflicts and maintain healthy connections.

7. Engage in Continuous Learning: Commit to lifelong learning and personal development to expand your knowledge, skills, and perspec-

tives. Stay curious, open-minded, and adaptable, embracing new opportunities for growth and self-improvement.

8. Prioritize Self-Care: Make self-care a priority in your daily routine, nurturing your physical, mental, and emotional well-being. Practice mindfulness, relaxation techniques, and stress management strategies to maintain balance.

9. Stay Active and Healthy: Take care of your physical health by exercising regularly, nutritious eating habits, and adequate rest and relaxation. Physical activity can boost mood, energy levels, and overall well being helping you to pursue your goals.

10. Trust Your Intuition: Listen to your inner wisdom and intuition as you navigate your path to freedom and fulfillment. Trust yourself to make decisions that align with your values, aspirations, and authentic self, even if they may not be popular or conventional.

By remaining resilient against external influences and staying true to yourself, you can pursue a career, develop skills, cultivate emotional intelligence, and nurture your overall well-being with confidence and determination. Remember that your journey to freedom is uniquely yours, and you can create the life you desire on your terms.

"In the depths of adversity lies the opportunity for greatness. Embrace your challenges, for they are the stepping stones to your triumph."
- Unknown

It's Not Over, Keep Moving
ForWARD...

You are the captain of your SHIP, so set Sail...

Live Live, Live On...the You that you have yet to meet is waiting on you on the other side.

CHAPTER 10

"Are You Ready for a Fresh Start?"

This marks the beginning of a new journey, a new experience where you allow yourself to be free, to realign to what you want beyond these walls. When I say ready for a fresh start, I mean ready to embrace the new you. Yes, there will be obstacles, setbacks, and closed doors along the way, but remember, those are not your doors, and that's perfectly OK. Our goal in this new chapter of life and this book is to help empower you from within. Changing everyday habits that can determine the state of our lives for better or worse is no easy task, especially when we still have those daunting words of inadequacy and self-doubt. But I am here to tell you to take care of your well-being and mind, how you talk to yourself, and **to be kind to your mind.**

If you're anything like me, you sometimes decide it's time to start fresh. You resolve to let go of old habits, ways of thinking, and behaviors that no longer serve you. You want to embark on a new and refreshing journey, freeing and forgiving. But you need to replace those old routines with new ones to do that.

As you embark on this journey, expect to be filled with optimism and determination. You'll create a list of resolutions, each a testament to your commitment to self-improvement. You'll reassure yourself that things will be different this time—that you'll be better, stronger, and more resilient. And indeed, you will emerge from the confines of your mind, ready to embrace the possibilities that lie ahead.

It's essential to recognize that starting over is perfectly okay, armed with the wisdom gained from past experiences and an open mind ready to rewrite your story. Remember, your mistakes do not dictate your future. Instead, they serve as stepping stones toward personal growth and transformation. So, with courage in your heart and determination in your soul, dare to rebuild, reinvent, and create the future you envision. Your journey begins now.

"Embrace the canvas of life with a new perspective, for within every fresh start lies the blueprint of invaluable life lessons."

"Starting over may feel daunting, but the journey is worth every step. Beyond the walls we've built, our minds should not be imprisoned by past experiences or setbacks. Instead, view them as the fuel that ignites new beginnings. Your hiccups have added new wings; now soar high because you deserve it.

Remember, embarking on a fresh start comes with numerous benefits. It offers growth, self-discovery, and the chance to create your desired life. By starting over, you open doors to new possibilities, experiences, and relationships that can enrich your life in ways you never imagined.

To help you get started, here's a checklist:

1. Reflect on past experiences: Acknowledge what you've learned and how it has shaped you.
2. Set clear intentions: Define what you want to achieve and why it matters.
3. Let go of fear: Embrace uncertainty as a gateway to growth and transformation.
4. Cultivate a positive mindset: Focus on possibilities rather than limitations.
5. Surround yourself with support: Seek guidance from mentors, friends, or support groups who uplift and encourage you.
6. Take consistent action: Break down your goals into manageable steps and commit to daily actions towards them.
7. Practice self-compassion: Be kind to yourself on this journey and celebrate progress, no matter how small.

By adopting this mindset shift and following these steps, you can break free from the constraints of the past and live a life filled with purpose, joy, and fulfillment. You have the power within you to rewrite your story and build the future you deserve. So, spread your wings and soar towards your dreams, for the sky is the limit!"

"Release the shackles of the imprisonment mindset, and watch as your spirit soars with wings unburdened, free, and clear."

You deserve to reinvent yourself. This time, you are free to be.

Reflecting on my own journey, I realize how quickly my life passed by, overshadowed by struggles with mental health and a lack of safe spaces to express myself authentically. I didn't have a space where I could open up and be myself otherwise without being judged. I allowed the opinions of others to dim my own light as I didn't want to show all of me due to fear of rejection. I want you to know that you deserve to be free from such constraints so that you can connect with your tribe and attract those that truly deserve to be in your presence and allow you to be your authentic self.

Reinventing yourself means tapping into the potential of the future you have yet to unleash. It's about giving yourself permission to live life on your terms, surrounded by supportive resources, communities, and people who resonate with your authenticity. As we conclude this chapter, it's an opportunity to create spaces where we can heal, set boundaries, and prioritize our well-being.

Letting go of the guilt and understanding that you two need time with yourself are crucial steps in this journey.

I ran so many red lights without pausing to breathe. But as I finish this chapter, which has been so challenging to write, I recognize that God wanted to show me that perfection is not the goal; sharing this with others is the key.

Be mindful of how you treat yourself and others; remember the importance of rest. In the final sections of this book, I will share some health and wellness tips along with some questions to guide you on your path. And always remember that we're not alone on this earth; we don't have to journey alone. As Charles Darwin once said, "It isn't the strongest species that survives, neither the most intelligent, but rather that which adapts best to change."

Navigating life's challenges and helping others, whether it's our community, family, or children, requires us to learn how to surpass the limits set by our minds. Fear often holds us captive, preventing us from finding solutions to these problems. It's important to let go of fear and learn to live without it. If we allow worry to take root in our minds, we can't solve problems using the same mindset that created them.

That's all I have to say for now. One of the hardest things to do is to be open-minded when you're in pain and in times of darkness, when you can't see the light at the end of the tunnel, and when exploring ideas that challenge your usual way of thinking. Our brains, though small in size, hold immense power and complexity. Treating our minds with kindness and compassion is essential, as we often become our harshest critics. By reframing our thoughts and seeking help when needed, we can break free from self-imposed limitations and live authentically. Each breath we take reminds us to let go of what no longer serves us.

Surviving has a lot to do with the capacity to solve problems, make decisions, face challenges, and even learn from your mistakes. It took me almost 17 years to truly forgive myself for one mistake that held me captive for 11 months. But every day, I thank God for the experience, which allowed me to come out in the right mind, ready to move forward and do better.

Embracing change and maintaining a positive attitude are crucial components of growth. Conducting a personal SWOT analysis allows us to assess where we are and identify areas for improvement. Reinventing ourselves requires deep introspection, honest conversations, and a willingness to let go of the past.

Remember, each person's journey of self-reinvention is unique. Not everyone will understand or support our path, but surrounding ourselves with healed individuals who align with our values can provide invaluable support. Never stop challenging yourself to grow and evolve despite doubts or setbacks.

Our minds, like software, are shaped by our experiences. Addressing past traumas and breaking free from mental stagnation allows us to unlock our true potential. As Lao Tzu wisely said, "Who can make muddy water clear? Let it be still, and it will gradually become clear." Let's embark on this journey of self-discovery and reinvention with courage and determination, trusting that clarity will come with time.

"You are the only person you need to be good enough for."

Our view of ourselves is pivotal. Comparing ourselves to others can rob us of joy and make us feel inadequate. Our past experiences, especially those in childhood, can shape our unconscious beliefs, which are deeply ingrained convictions that cannot be disputed. These beliefs can lead to feelings of uncertainty and inadequacy.

However, we must learn to love ourselves and use tools to break free from our limiting beliefs. We must focus on what we want instead of what we fear and have faith in ourselves as we reinvent ourselves. Remember that you are enough; anyone who doesn't support you should be left behind as you dance in the rain with your umbrella shielding you.

Reinventing oneself means changing external circumstances and transforming our internal landscape, rewriting our narrative, and embracing our worthiness. Comparison is the thief of joy, and it can leave us feeling inadequate and diminish our sense of self. However, the truth is that we are the only people we need to be good enough for.

Our past experiences, especially those rooted in childhood, can shape unconscious beliefs that perpetuate feelings of unworthiness. It's essential to recognize that these beliefs are not facts but merely interpretations of past events. Although the pain of the past may have kept us running, always seeking validation or escape, now is the time to pause, reflect, and recognize our worthiness.

Reinvention begins with self-love and acceptance. We must love every aspect of ourselves, including the messy, loud, wild, and imperfect. It is about embracing our uniqueness and allowing ourselves to dance freely in the rain, regardless of who may disapprove.

To embark on this journey of reinvention, we must focus on what we desire rather than succumb to our fears. Although fear may accompany new beginnings, it is through faith and perseverance that we can overcome it. As we say yes to ourselves, we bid farewell to fear and welcome a future filled with self-discovery, growth, and fulfillment. Remember that you can achieve anything you set your mind to, and with perseverance and determination, nothing can stop you.

> **"Embrace the power within you to rewrite your story, reinvent your path, and reclaim your worth. In the journey of self-reinvention lies the liberation of self-acceptance."**

Let It Go

Free yourself from guilt, clutter, stress, and negative self-talk hang-ups make this year your best year yet.

To live our best lives, we must consider learning the art of letting go. Freeing ourselves from the shackles of guilt, clutter, stress, and negative self-talk is essential to embrace the beauty that surrounds us. Finding Beauty in an ordinary walk is a journey. As we step beyond the walls that once confined us, the chapter unfolds with a call to live again, learn from life's lessons woven into our narrative, and find beauty in the ordinary walk. It's a journey of self-discovery, transformation, and the unwavering commitment to nurture the most important relationship - with oneself.

> *"Letting go doesn't mean you don't care about someone anymore. It's just realizing that the only person you really have control over is yourself.*
> *- Deborah Reber*

Living Again: Embrace the New View of Life

Permission to Change Course: Give yourself liberating permission to change your course. Life is fluid, and growth often requires a shift in direction. The foundation for such changes is acceptance and the support of acknowledging one's innate capacity to redefine one's path.

Commitment to Self-Nurturing:

Central to this chapter is the unwavering commitment to nurturing the relationship with oneself. Self-care is not a luxury but a necessity in the hustle and bustle of life. It involves treating oneself with kindness, embracing imperfections, and recognizing the inherent worthiness of self-love.

The Challenge of Embracing Today: Staying present is a gift

Embracing the Hard Moments

Acknowledge that life is a tapestry of moments, both easy and challenging. Embrace what comes hard today, for it is often in facing challenges that we unearth our deepest strengths. Each challenge is an opportunity for growth and resilience.

Falling in Love with the Process: Encourage you to love the transformation process. Transformation is not always adorned with butterflies and dancing; it's a journey that involves setbacks, introspection, and the resilience to keep moving forward. It's about finding beauty in the unfolding story, no matter its twists and turns.

Guilt weighs heavy on the heart, chaining us to past mistakes and regrets. But in letting go of guilt, we liberate ourselves to move forward with grace and forgiveness, allowing room for growth and self-compassion.

Clutter fills not only our physical space but also our minds, hindering clarity and peace. Decluttering our lives creates space for new experiences, ideas, and opportunities to blossom, leading to a more fulfilling and intentional existence.

> *"Sometimes the most productive thing you can do is relax."*
> **- Mark Black**

Stress is a constant companion in our modern lives, but it doesn't have to dictate our well-being. Learning to let go of stress involves surrendering to the present moment, practicing mindfulness, and prioritizing self-care to cultivate inner calm and resilience.

Negative self-talk is a silent saboteur, eroding our confidence and self-worth. By releasing the grip of negative thoughts and beliefs, we open ourselves up to a world of possibilities, embracing our inherent worthiness and potential for greatness.

> *"By letting it go, it all gets done. The world is won by those who let it go. But when you try and try, the world is beyond winning.*
> **- Lao Tzu**

As we embark on this journey of letting go, we reclaim our power to shape our destinies and make this year our best. With each release, we uncover the beauty in the ordinary walk of life, finding joy, peace, and fulfillment in every step forward.

On this journey, we call life

As we continue this journey today, let us take a moment to reflect on the path that has led us to this point. Each of us has walked through our own trials, faced our challenges, and emerged stronger and wiser on the other side. Today, we stand on the threshold of a new chapter, ready to embrace the beauty in ordinary life. Life, as we know, is a journey—a journey filled with twists and turns, highs and lows, victories and defeats. But through it all, there is a constant call to live again, to learn from the lessons that life has woven into our narrative, and to find beauty in the most ordinary moments.

Today, I share the importance of **letting go** —letting go of the burdens that weigh us down, the clutter that fills our lives, the stress that consumes our minds, and the negative self-talk that holds us back. For it is in letting go that we truly free ourselves to live our best lives.

Guilt, my friends, is a heavy burden to bear. It chains us to past mistakes and regrets, preventing us from moving forward with grace and forgiveness. But in letting go of guilt, we liberate ourselves to embrace new opportunities for growth and self-compassion.

Clutter, both physical and mental, clouds our vision and stifles our creativity. But by decluttering our lives, we create space for new experiences, ideas, and possibilities to enter.

Stress, that relentless companion of modern life, threatens to overwhelm us at every turn. But by learning to let go of stress, we cultivate inner calm and resilience, allowing us to navigate life's challenges gracefully and easily.

And negative self-talk, that insidious voice of doubt and criticism, chips away at our confidence and self-worth. But by releasing the grip of negative thoughts and beliefs, we reclaim our power and embrace our inherent worthiness.

My beautiful souls, as we embark on this journey of letting go, let us remember that we hold the key to our happiness and fulfillment. With each release, we uncover the beauty in ordinary life, finding joy, peace, and fulfillment in every step forward.

So let us dare to let go of the past, of the clutter, of the stress, and of the negativity that holds us back. Let us make this year our best year yet as we embrace the beauty of the ordinary walk and live each day to the fullest.

Words of Wisdom and Affirmations:

Navigating the Journey: **"In the transformation journey, expect butterflies and storms. Yet, navigating through storms gives us the strength to soar to new heights."**

Resetting the Mind and Rejuvenating the Spirit:

May the new month reset your mind to rejuvenate your spirit. Every day, I learn that not everything requires a response; not every action needs my reaction or attention. Let go of your ego when you're trying to recreate your life. They say that the only way to do so is to love yourself in the way you spend time with others and yourself in that moment of life. Looking back over my life, I appreciate where I've been and how far I've come.

> *"Life is not a solo act. It's a grand ensemble where every experience and connection weaves a unique melody. Embrace the harmony of your journey, and let the notes of courage, wisdom, and joy resonate with the beauty that is your life.*
> - Florida Scott-Maxwell

Exercises

Please close your eyes and think about a stressful situation you're facing at the moment, whether it's small or large. Notice where you feel tension when you think about this tough situation. Finding a spot might take a minute—good places to check are your jaws, shoulders, belly, chest, and throat.

Once you've identified the spot where you feel tension, rest your hand on that area and inhale deeply. Imagine the breath flowing into and around the tense spot, and then exhale naturally, letting go of any tightness. Repeat this process a few times, allowing your breath to guide you deeper into relaxation. If you notice tension in more than one spot, move your hand and your breath to another area and repeat the process. Then, when you're ready, relax with your eyes closed and your hands in your lap, feeling the newfound softness in those areas.

You can do this exercise anytime, anywhere—even with your eyes open and even if you're unsure what the source of your tension is. Breathing into tightness and softening creates a gentle space for attention and relaxation, allowing you to release the stress that weighs you down.

My Yogi community has taught me the power of breath to accept where we are, change our perspectives, and look at things differently. I wanted to share this practice with you to invite you to sit in stillness and find space for yourself, whether it's outdoors, in your own private Zen room, like I have created for myself, or with friends.

This is one of those moments when you can take the time to let go, release the tension that binds you, and reconnect with the peace and tranquility that resides within. As you breathe in deeply, let yourself surrender to the present moment, knowing that you have the power to find calm amidst the chaos.

Remember, with each breath, you are creating space for healing, clarity, and a renewed sense of inner peace. So, take this moment to breathe, let go, and embrace the beauty of simply being.

Do more of what makes you happy and *Live Live Live!*

"Embrace life with open arms, letting its challenges sculpt you into the resilient, courageous soul you're destined to become. Every hurdle you face is an opportunity for growth, and every joy reminds you of life's beauty. Remember, if it doesn't challenge you, it won't change you. So, seize each moment, learn from every experience, and craft your unique path to greatness. Live passionately, love fiercely, and thrive abundantly!" Remember, beauty is the moment you decide to be yourself #Dare2liftit

Here are some tips for living a fulfilling and balanced life

1. Count Your Blessings: Take time each day to reflect on what you're grateful for. Cultivating an attitude of gratitude can shift your perspective and bring more joy into your life.

2. Be Honest with Yourself: Self-awareness is key to personal growth. Be honest about your strengths, weaknesses, and areas for improvement. Embrace your authenticity and strive to be the best version of yourself.

3. Say No to Stress: Learn to recognize when you're feeling overwhelmed and take steps to manage stress effectively. Practice relaxation techniques such as deep breathing, meditation, or yoga to calm your mind and body.

4. It's OK to Ask for Help: Don't be afraid to reach out for support when needed. Whether it's from friends, family, or a professional, seeking help is a sign of strength, not weakness.

5. Nurture Your Spirituality: Connect with your inner self and explore practices that nourish your soul, whether it's meditation, prayer, or

spending time in nature. Cultivating a spiritual practice can bring peace and purpose to your life.

6. Take Care of Your Body: Your body is your temple, so treat it with love and respect. Eat nutritious foods, exercise regularly, and prioritize sleep to maintain your physical health and well-being.

7. Confront Bad Habits and Add New Healthy Habits: Identify unhealthy habits that may be holding you back and take steps to replace them with positive ones. Set achievable goals and celebrate your progress along the way.

8. Give Generously Without Expectation: Practice kindness and generosity towards others without expecting anything in return. The act of giving can bring immense joy and fulfillment to both the giver and the receiver.

9. Have Hard Conversations and Stop Avoiding Confrontation: Addressing difficult issues head-on is essential for healthy relationships and personal growth. Be courageous and willing to have uncomfortable conversations in order to resolve conflicts and move forward.

10. Keep Your Word and Be Careful About Commitments: Integrity is key to building trust and credibility. Honor your commitments and be mindful of the promises you make.

Make sure your actions align with your values and priorities.

11. Eat Better for a Better Life: Fuel your body with nourishing foods that support your health and vitality. Prioritize whole foods, fruits, vegetables, and plenty of water to fuel your body and mind.

12. Talk It Out: Communication is the cornerstone of healthy relationships. Don't keep difficult emotions bottled up inside. Instead, express yourself openly and honestly and encourage others to do the same.

13. Have Fun: Embrace your inner child and make time for play and spontaneity. Whether splashing in the waves or dancing in the rain, remember to have fun and enjoy the simple pleasures of life.

14. Know How Much is Enough: Strive for balance and contentment in all areas of your life. Focus on maximizing what you have rather than constantly chasing more. True quality of life comes from finding joy and fulfillment in the present moment.

15. Enhance Your Relationships: Invest time and effort into building meaningful connections with others. Practice active listening, empathy, and compassion, and be generous with your

love and support. Remember to create space for others to grow and thrive alongside you.

16. Today is the day to build the tomorrow you want live out loud.

MINDFULNESS MOMENTS

Closing the Chapter: Beyond the Walls

As we reach the end of this chapter, let us reflect on the journey we've undertaken together. The seeds of transformation planted within us have sprouted, enabling us to outgrow old patterns and pains and move toward the authentic direction of our souls. I encourage you always to be true to yourself, to spread light wherever you go, and to keep your head up, knowing that you're destined for more.

Cultivating the Gift Within Each of us possesses a unique gift - a special ability that we can develop over time. This gift is a precious endowment bestowed upon us, waiting to be nurtured and cultivated. Forgiveness is the key to allowing our true essence to flourish. Take stock of your life, identify elements that no longer serve your evolution, and break free to be the best version of yourself. Yes, place it where you see it fit; trust your judgment.

Embracing Life After the Unforeseen: Life's journey may lead us to unexpected places, prompting questions like "How did I get here?" and "What happened?" These queries reflect untold stories and unexplored depths. However, the real challenge lies in responding to the present with a resounding "Now what?" Life keeps going, relentless and unyielding, weaving our past into the fabric of our interactions. Acknowledge your inherent strengths and let them become the building blocks for a resilient foundation.

No Longer Hiding: Create a sanctuary within yourself where you no longer need to hide. Embrace your scars as badges of resilience and reveal your authentic self, opening yourself to the possibilities that lie ahead.

Openness to a New Future: Craft a new chapter filled with resilience, self-love, and intentional living. Be open to life's infinite possibilities and embark on an exciting exploration of what comes next.

Healing and Intentional Living: Commit to healing, understanding, and intentional living. Embrace self-awareness and self-love and move away from the victim mentality. Trust the process and be open to guidance from unexpected sources.

A Triumvirate of Self-Empowerment: Acknowledge, love, and bet on yourself. Recognize the intricacies and imperfections of your journey and love yourself unconditionally. Bet on your incredible strength and capacity for growth.

So, as you stand at the crossroads of "Now what?" Remember, the journey is not just about understanding what happened but crafting what happens next. Life's puzzle aligns into a beautiful mosaic when lived intentionally and with a deep belief in your potential for greatness. Keep moving forward with courage, grace, and an unwavering belief in the power of your dreams. The best is yet to come.

> **"Sometimes you wake up, sometimes the fall kills you, and sometimes when you fall, you fly."**
> **- Neil Gaiman**

Do you start your day with positive thoughts?

Evaluate them, adjust them if needed, and keep moving forward. What do you normally think about when you first wake up? Are your thoughts positive or negative? Are you usually excited about your day, or do you dread starting it? How do you normally set the tone for your date? Tell me or tell yourself what you will release in this new journey.

_____
_____
_____
_____
_____
_____
_____
_____
_____
_____
_____
_____
_____
_____

Start your day with a positive mindset. Evaluate your thoughts and adjust them if necessary to keep yourself moving forward. Focus on the possibilities of the day ahead, be excited about what's to come and take charge of setting the tone for your day. Release any negativity and embrace the new day with confidence and enthusiasm.

Are your relationships adding positive or negative value?

Mindfulness and Journaling Exercise:

Take a moment to pause and reflect on the relationships in your life. Are the people you surround yourself with adding value to your life, or are they draining you emotionally and mentally? Have you felt exhausted or demotivated after spending time with certain individuals while feeling recharged and inspired around others?

Grab your journal, and let's delve deeper into this reflection exercise:

1. **Positive Impact Relationships:**
   - List the people in your life who positively impact you. These could be friends, family members, mentors, or colleagues.
   - Reflect on why you feel positive about these relationships. What specific behaviors, attitudes, or actions do these individuals exhibit that contribute to their positive impact on your life?
   - Write down moments when these individuals have uplifted, supported, or inspired you to be

your best self.

2. **Negative Impact Relationships:**
- Now, list the people in your life who have had a negative impact on you. These could be individuals who drain your energy, bring negativity into your life, or hinder your personal growth.
- Reflect on why you feel negatively about these relationships. What specific behaviors, attitudes, or actions do these individuals exhibit that contribute to their negative impact on your life?
- Write examples of moments when these individuals have made you feel exhausted, demotivated, or emotionally drained.

3. **Exploring Emotions and Boundaries:**
- Take some time to explore your emotions surrounding these relationships. How do you feel when you're around these individuals? Do you feel supported, valued, respected, or anxious, frustrated, or invalidated?
- Reflect on whether you need to set boundaries or have conversations to protect your well-being and maintain healthy relationships.
- Consider how you can prioritize spending time with those who uplift and inspire you while also setting boundaries with those who drain your energy and contribute to negativity in your life.

4. **Setting Intentions for Change:**
   - Based on your reflections, set intentions for cultivating more positive and nourishing relationships. This could involve spending more time with supportive individuals, setting boundaries with toxic relationships, or seeking new connections aligning with your values and goals.
   - Write down actionable steps you can take to nurture and strengthen the positive relationships in your life while also creating healthy boundaries and distance from negative influences.

Remember, the people we surround ourselves with significantly impact our overall well-being and happiness. By cultivating mindfulness and awareness in our relationships, we can create a supportive and uplifting environment that empowers us to thrive beyond the walls of our past experiences.

Reflecting on Daily Habits and Actions:

Take a moment to reflect on your daily life. What actions do you find yourself repeating the most? While having a routine can provide structure to our lives, it's essential to examine whether the habits we've formed are contributing to our personal growth and well-being or simply consuming our time and energy.

Grab your journal, and let's make a list of the actions and habits you engage in every day:

1. **Morning Routine:**
   - What do you typically do when you wake up in the morning? Do you have a morning routine that sets the tone for your day?
   - Reflect on whether your morning habits align with your goals and values. Are you starting your day in a way that promotes positivity, productivity, and self-care?
2. **Work or School Tasks:**
   - Think about your tasks throughout your work or school day. What actions do you repeat daily in these environments?
   - Consider how these tasks contribute to your personal and professional growth. Are you actively learning, challenging yourself, and striving for excellence in your work or studies?
3. **Health and Wellness Practices:**
   - Reflect on your habits related to health and wellness. This could include exercise, nutrition, hydration, sleep, and self-care activities.
   - Evaluate whether these habits support your overall well-being and vitality. Are you prioritizing activities that nourish your body, mind, and spirit?
4. **Social Interactions:**
   - Consider the interactions you have with others throughout the day. Who do you spend time with, and how do these interactions make you feel?

- Reflect on whether your social habits contribute to positive connections, support networks, and personal growth. Are you surrounding yourself with people who uplift and inspire you?

5. **Technology and Media Consumption:**
- Think about how you engage with technology and media on a daily basis. How much time do you spend on devices or consuming content?
- Reflect on whether your habits are enhancing or detracting from your quality time. Are you using technology mindfully and intentionally, or is it consuming your time and attention?

6. **Self-Reflection and Growth Practices:**
- Consider whether you prioritize time for self-reflection and personal growth activities. Do you engage in practices like journaling, meditation, or goal setting?
- Reflect on how these habits contribute to your self-awareness, resilience, and growth mindset. Are you actively investing in your personal development and learning from your experiences?

As you reflect on your daily habits and actions, consider how they align with your values, goals, and aspirations. Are there any habits you'd like to cultivate or change to better support your personal growth and well-being? Use this reflection as an opportunity to make conscious choices about how you spend your time and energy each day, empowering yourself to live the best life possible.

Meet the Author

Matilde Hernandez is a Certified Personal Growth and Wellness coach, and community leader who has inspired many through her small business, All In One Cleaning Service. She is also certified at the highest level as an international John Maxwell speaker trainer and a DISC behavior analysis consultant.

Matilde Hernandez is a dedicated professional committed to fostering personal growth and well-being. With a bachelor's degree in business administration from American Intercontinental University and a master's degree and currently a student of **performance psychology** supporting individuals in healing from the inside out. She helps them on their wellness journey to reach their highest self.

This involves setting strategic business goals to aid people in their journey of reconstruction after experiencing trauma, breakups, or other difficulties. Matilde understands that life's challenges are unavoidable, yet she considers them opportunities for personal development and resilience.

Her foundation course, Dare 2 Lift It, was created to support building individuals, offering a roadmap for personal growth and wellness. The course includes behavioral health analysis, business setup support, online coaching, and programs aimed at self-improvement. Matilde's message to the world is clear: "You deserve a healthy, positive, successful life. You deserve to start living again." For her corporate clients, she delivers stress management and effective communication training. These programs help restore, rejuvenate, and foster team building and effective organizational communication.

Mother of two, born in the Dominican Republic and raised in Miami, Fl. Her journey is fueled by her passion for adding value to others' lives and making a difference in her community. She actively works with nonprofits, focusing on youth development and providing skills training for young mothers.

Her mantra, "It Starts With You," emphasizes the importance of personal responsibility in creating positive change. Whether it's within families, communities, or schools, she believes that everyone possesses the power to be the catalyst for transformation. She encourages others to recognize the light within themselves and use it as a tool to uplift those around them.

Let's Connect

IG: Dare2liftit
Unpackthatbefreepodcast

Website: Dare2liftit.com

LinkedIn:
https://www.linkedin.com/in/matilde-hernandez-mba-6b96aa25

Website: Dare2liftit.com

www.ingramcontent.com/pod-product-compliance
Lightning Source LLC
Chambersburg PA
CBHW051942160426
43198CB00013B/2259